# PLANNING
for
# CHRISTIAN EDUCATION
## FORMATION

*For Tom and Sammi
on their first year.*

*With loving appreciation for
Connie, Kristin, Lauren, and Alexandra,
my parents and extended family,
and the congregations and Christian friends
who have been my companions in life and ministry.*

# PLANNING
### for
# CHRISTIAN EDUCATION
## FORMATION

## *A Community*
## *of Faith Approach*

## Israel Galindo • Marty C. Canaday

**CHALICE**
PRESS

ST. LOUIS, MISSOURI

Scripture quotations, unless otherwise marked, are taken from the HOLY BIBLE, NEW INTERNATIONAL VERSION®. NIV®. Copyright © 1973, 1978, 1984 by International Bible Society. Used by permission of Zondervan Publishing House. All rights reserved.

Bible quotations marked NRSV are from the *New Revised Standard Version Bible,* copyright 1989, Division of Christian Education of the National Council of the Churches of Christ in the United States of America. Used by permission. All rights reserved.

Scripture quotations marked (CEV) are taken from the *Contemporary English Version.* Copyright © 1991, 1992, 1995 by American Bible Society. Used by Permission.

Cover art: Photodisc
Cover and interior design: Elizabeth Wright

## ChalicePress.com

EPUB: 978-08272-30187    EPDF: 978-08272-30194

### Library of Congress Cataloging-in-Publication Data

Galindo, Israel.
  Planning for Christian education formation : a community of faith approach / Israel Galindo, Marty C. Canaday.
      p. cm.
  Includes bibliographical references (p. 135).
  ISBN 978-0-8272-3011-8
  1. Christian education. 2. Spiritual formation. I. Canaday, Marty C. II. Title.

BV1471.3.G355 2010
268–dc22

                                                              2009047117

Printed in United States of America

# Contents

***Special acknowledgments to:***

Judy Bennett, Steve Booth, Bob Dibble, Vanessa Ellison,
Mike Harton, Terry Maples, Nathan Taylor,
and Fred Skaggs

for their help in making this a better book.

# Introduction

This book will help church education leaders address the following questions: Does your church know how Christian faith is formed? Does your church have an intentional process for developing an effective Christian education ministry? How do you determine what contributes to and what impedes effective Christian formation in your congregation? What informing theology guides your church's education practice? Do you know the differences between program-centered approaches and a community-of-faith approach to Christian education?

This book was born during a conversation. The authors of this book work in different contexts in the field of religious education. One is a congregational Christian educator engaged in the practice of religious education in the local parish. The other is a seminary professor who teaches religious education and congregational studies. Both consult with congregational staff and lay leaders. During a conversation they became aware that one of the most frequent cries for help they receive is about how to plan and organize the education ministry in the local church. Often these phone calls come from recent seminary graduates who failed to have the foresight to take any Christian education courses during their formal seminary training. Many other phone calls or e-mails come from laypersons or newly hired church staff persons who do not have training or experience in education planning and organization. Most of these persons practice Christian education by maintaining existing education programs and structures, and ordering a series of convenient published curricular or program resources. The time comes when they realize that their un-systematic approach is ineffective. Programs wane, people lose interest and stop attending, teachers get discouraged, and the church's education program gets stale and "stuck."

Many churches fail to understand the unique *corporate* nature of Christian education formation. Few congregational education leaders seem to actually understand what "faith formation" is and how to plan

1

and organize an education program with that orientation. Traditional approaches to congregational Christian education have tended to use "schooling-instructional" models and methods for educating in faith. We will argue that instruction is both important and necessary, but is limited in its ability to address the dynamics of how congregations form faith. Many churches have not only kept the old education wineskins, they've also not been able to discover new wine. They perpetuate a benign education program that makes little impact on participants.

Maria Harris helped redefine the concept of curriculum.[1] Her central message is we are what we do. Our understanding of Christian education and the way we plan the education programs of the church will determine the extent to which we can help persons be formed into "Christlikeness."

Morton Kelsey suggested that Christian education may be more effective if it used religious principles in teaching Christianity.[2] This book contends that most congregational leaders lack a theological framework and thus rely on educational approaches that are not congruent with how faith actually develops in a corporate faith community context. To be effective, Christian education must use educational approaches congruent to its nature and purpose.

We are advocating a different way of approaching the Christian education ministry in the local church. The *Christian education formation approach* takes seriously two realities in congregations. First, while congregations organize themselves in institutional forms, they are by nature communities of faith. Congregations must make it possible for members to "be in community" while being responsible stewards of their institutions. Second, formation, more so than schooling, brings about spiritual growth for individuals and communities of faith. *Christian education formation* represents an approach that takes these two often paradoxical realities into account without denying either.

Thomas Groome told religious educators, "If we only want people to 'learn about' religious traditions, then schooling is enough. But if we want them to "learn from" a tradition, perhaps to ground their spiritual identity in it, then schools and formal programs, although vital, will not be sufficient."[3] The growing interest in spiritual formation, and its attention to the dynamics of faith formation, offers a more hopeful way for congregations to help their members grow in faith.

The premise of this book is that congregations, by their nature, are authentic communities of faith. Therefore, congregational leaders need to plan and organize the ways of learning for the congregation congruent to its nature. The framework provided for planning Christian education formation from a faith community approach includes the following:

1. The use of the Christian Church Year as an organizing framework for planning and designing formational education programs and events;
2. The organization of an effective *Christian Education Leadership Team;*
3. The creation of effective administrative and organizational processes and structures;
4. The theological assessment of the cultural context of the congregation's practices in light of the community of faith perspective;
5. The use of education approaches congruent with corporate, communal, and individual faith formation.

This is a practical handbook for planning an effective Christian education ministry for community and individual formation. The principles identified in the book will help your education leaders move beyond being uncritical consumers of educational products that perpetuate ineffective programs that are not congruent with the nature of corporate and individual faith formation. You and your education leaders will gain a new lens that will allow you to minister more effectively in your unique education leadership roles.

Five premises inform this book's education approach:

- First, a congregation is an authentic community of faith. It shapes the faith of its members in the ways that communities do—not in the way a school does.
- Second, for learning in the domain of faith two principles apply: (1) you learn to do what you do and not something else that you have acquired intellectually or emotionally, and (2) *how* you learn is *what* you learn.
- Third, the goal of Christian education formation in the congregational setting is the formation of individuals into the likeness of Christ as members of a community of faith.
- Fourth, the result of effective Christian education formation is discipleship: living a life of obedience to God and responding to God's call to personal spiritual growth and service to and through the Church.
- Fifth, effective Christian education formation is *real* education. Leaders must give attention to sound education processes:

identifying program goals; planning objectives; conducting assessments; and practicing supervision, administration, and planning.

The book consists of three parts. Part I will provide an orientation to the perspective of planning for Christian education formation in the congregational setting. This part will provide the theological framework for understanding your congregation as an authentic community of faith. This foundation will help you refocus the Christian education enterprise in your church from programs and schooling models to the communal and formation model.

Part II provides the "nuts and bolts" for planning and organizing a Christian education formation program from a faith community approach. You will examine the following topics: the organization and work of your leadership team, how to create a program structure using the Christian Church Year, and how to select appropriate educational approaches to meet your education goals.

Part III will address two critical areas of education practice: education assessment and how to address the issues related to changing your congregation's culture and practice as you move toward the community-of-faith approach.

# PART I: Orientation to Planning Perspectives

*The Theological Framework of a Christian Faith Community*

# 1

# A Community-of-Faith Approach to Christian Education Formation

Few Christian educators will admit that the way we have been educating people in faith over the last fifty years is not very effective. Even fewer will admit that the current practices of the local congregation have failed to result in the kind of spiritual maturity we desire to see in our church members. The unspoken truth of Christian education today is that the educational practices of the past have not served us well in shaping persons in "Christlikeness" because they run counter to the way people need to be educated in faith. A better way to facilitate the process of Christian education is congruent with how Christian faith is actually formed in the context of a community of faith.

The community-of-faith approach posits that the members of a congregation are formed in the context of its culture as they participate in the corporate practices of faith. In other words, the congregation itself, as a type of community of faith, forms the faith of its members. Robert K. Martin wrote, "Education must be broadly conceived to include the relatively implicit means by which people learn even without knowing that they are learning."[1]

A Search Institute report titled *Effective Christian Education: A National Study of Protestant Congregations* suggested seven climates of congregational life that help foster faith maturity:[2]

### Seven Climates of Congregational Life

1. *Warmth*–Friendliness and welcoming atmosphere
2. *Thinking*–Intellectual engagement consisting of thinking and discussion
3. *Caring*–Experiencing the care of others
4. *Service Orientation*–Involvement of members in outreach and ministry
5. *Worship*–Variety, flow, and involvement in worship
6. *Parent Education*–Helping parents strengthen skills as religious educators at home
7. *Education*–Strong and vibrant education program for all ages

Congregations must provide for these seven climates to effectively educate in faith. The study found that Christian education is the most important practice within congregational life for helping people grow in their faith. "Done well, it has the potential beyond any other congregational influence to deepen faith and commitment. Knowledge of its importance makes the need for educational revitalization all the more urgent."[3] The right changes can improve education effectiveness in congregations and help their members grow in their faith. Every congregation, no matter how small, has within it the very resources needed to offer an effective Christian education formation program. "Ecclesial life *is* already constituted by relationship (*koinonia*), rituals and patterns of action (*leitourgia*), individual and corporate knowledge (*didache*), the ways we serve (*diaconia*), and the vision and purpose of our life together (*kerygma*)," claims Robert K. Martin.[4]

In recent years, the thirst for relevance in congregational life has given birth to changes in worship and music styles. Unfortunately, rather than seeing all aspects of congregational life as the local church's greatest education asset, many congregations are ignoring the research and trying to "fix" the church by offering diverse worship styles to divergent audiences. This clearly indicates that many congregational leaders do not appreciate the communal nature of the local congregation and how persons need to be educated in faith in a communal context. Isolating one part of congregational life from others, or one population group from others, in an attempt to reclaim the relevancy of church, or as an anxious response to predilections of taste, will not result in spiritual growth and Christian transformation.

## Schooling vs. Community Formation

Planning for Christian education formation from a community-of-faith approach will require a shift in our thinking about the nature of Christian education in the local church. If the church is to be effective in Christian education formation, it must be true to its nature. The chart below illustrates the shift that needs to happen. It depicts two contrasting approaches to religious education. The left column names universal education categories. These categories apply to any education enterprise: a university, a college, a seminary, a training program, a Christian elementary school, or a congregation's education program. Clarity about how these categories need to be applied will help determine the effectiveness of any particular education enterprise.

**Figure 1–1: Religious Instruction and Formation Education in Contrast**

| CATEGORIES | RELIGIOUS INSTRUCTION (Schooling Model) | FORMATION EDUCATION (Community-of-Faith Model) |
|---|---|---|
| Context | Classroom | Community of Faith |
| Content | Text or Creed | The Person of Jesus Christ |
| Approach | Didactic (instructional) | Relational |
| Outcome | Mastery of Content | Becoming in Relationship |
| Methods | Instruction | Dialogical |

The middle column depicts the appropriate ways of applying the categories in a school setting. The context for instruction is the classroom, an environment that naturally fosters the roles of teacher and student. The content of instruction is the particular text or creed under study—the Bible, a particular text or book, a topic of study, or a course of instruction. The appropriate educational approaches to use are didactic and instructional ways of teaching and learning. The effective practice of instruction requires the use of rigorous, specific, and measurable learning outcomes. Those academic outcomes are related to mastery of the content—understanding and application of concepts, comprehension of principles, evidence of critical thinking (analysis, synthesis, evaluation), etc.

By way of contrast, the right column depicts a community-of-faith approach to Christian education formation. The context in which educating in faith happens is the community of faith, the church. The content of a community of faith is its relationship with Jesus

Christ. This approach assumes you are a Christian by who you know, not by what you know. The appropriate approach in a communal context is relational, not didactic. The ultimate purpose of Christian teaching and learning is to lead persons to a relationship with a living person–Jesus Christ. The learning outcome for Christian formation is thus more about developing relationships than gaining knowledge, or, as Paul put it, to "grow up into him who is the Head, that is, Christ" (Eph. 4:15). The only methods that facilitate growth between persons are dialogical. Dialogical methods–friendships, mentoring, apprenticeships, discipleship–are those that promote deep sharing, mutual accountability, vulnerable transparency, and self-revelation. In Paul's words, "But [whoever] loves God is known by God" (1 Cor. 8:3) and, "[T]hen I shall know fully, even as I am fully known" (1 Cor. 13:12).[5]

Paradoxically, congregations, as authentic communities of faith according to their nature, have the assets to be effective in the faith formation of their members, but they consistently choose an education model that is primarily instructional in nature–an educational approach incongruent with both the nature of church and the way faith is formed. How a congregation answers the question, "Is a congregation by nature a school for religious education, or a community that shapes faith through shared communal life?" will determine how a congregation goes about its planning and what practices it provides to form and transform the lives of its members. This is the watershed question that will tilt congregational practice toward effectiveness or ineffectiveness in faith formation.

The evidence appears clear. Schooling approaches to Christian education are not effective for faith formation. To advocate a move from instructional approaches should not be construed as arguing for any less rigor or discipline in the practice of Christian education in the local church. Nor should it be interpreted as devaluing knowledge, critical thinking, or intellectual discipline. A mature faith is a critical faith–it can reflect on its experience and is not naïve. Padraic O'Hare put it, "More simply and succinctly, religious education must have a dual purpose: the evoking of devotion and the promotion of inquiry."[6]

### False Assumptions Lead to False Practices
A failure to understand and appreciate how faith is formed in the context of a community of faith can lead to ineffective practices in Christian education. False assumptions about educating in faith

lead to "false practices" in a church's education ministry. The first false assumption is that people can be schooled in faith. This false assumption confuses religious instruction with faith formation. Robert K. Martin asserts, "The primary context and means of educational activity is participation in the forms of ecclesial life."[7] The context in which faith formation happens is in a community of faith, not a "school." It is appropriate to "school" students in an educational institution, such as a school or seminary, but a congregation educates its members in faith through formation mediated by its culture and the quality of relationships cultivated within the community of faith.

The second false assumption is that the teacher is the agent for learning. This assumption fails to appreciate how learning actually happens, and also perpetuates the over-focus on instruction in the church's approach to Christian education formation. This leads to the practice of teaching-by-telling as the mode for learning faith. Teaching-by-telling does not work, because it does other people's thinking for them. Asked, "On any given Sunday, who is the person that has learned the most at the end of the lesson?" a group of church teachers always answers immediately: "The teacher!" Asked, "Why is that so?" they answer correctly: "Because the teacher studied the lesson." The next obvious question is, "Then why do we expect our students to learn when we deny them the very process that brings about learning?"

The learner is the agent of his or her own learning. Instead of allowing learners to engage in the *process of study* for themselves, we attempt to plant insight by teaching-by-telling. The result is the formation of passive learners who are perpetual "pupils" in the life of faith, perpetually dependent on a teacher for learning. The paradox here is that to be perpetually dependent on another for one's growth in the life of faith only ensures that one never will.[8]

A third false assumption is that children (and youth) cannot appreciate "adult" corporate worship experiences. This results in our removing children and youth from participating in the corporate worship service of the community of faith. This false assumption fails to appreciate the formative power of shared intergenerational experiences. Communal values are inculcated in the shared experience of corporate practices. Assuming that children and youth do not have the capacity to understand worship ignores two fundamental rules. First, "You learn to do what you do and not something else." The only way one learns to worship as a member of one's community of faith is by participating in corporate worship. Second, this assumption fails to appreciate that worship is not about "understanding." Worship is a corporate practice of obedience and an opportunity to experience the Holy through formative rituals of practice. To hold intellectual understanding as a criterion for the participation of children or youth (or adults for that matter) is misguided.

A community-of-faith approach to Christian education formation provides a broader epistemology of learning. It takes into account the importance of directly shared experiences as formative to faith and respects the importance of the intuitive acquisition of religious knowledge through participation in the life of faith.

The fourth false assumption commonly practiced in congregations is that the most effective way to educate in faith is through tightly age-graded and group-segregated educational programming. When congregations follow this practice, nearly all children's, youth, and adult educational activities occur in isolation from the rest of the community of faith—not to mention the unfortunate segregation of family members one from another as soon as they walk in the church doors. That is not how people learn in faith communities. Faith communities teach via corporate intergenerational, cross-generational, and intra-generational connections and relationships. Robert K. Martin states, "The educational ministry of a congregation should give greatest priority to engaging people in the fellowship, practices, and ministries of ecclesial life. Secondary forms of education, namely, instruction and other schooling practices, should support and intensify the participation of persons in the primary forms of ecclesial life."[9] So clearly, your congregation *should not* eliminate all classroom or age-graded programs. They serve their purposes. You *should* change the way you understand and practice Christian education formation by moving toward a community-of-faith approach—one informed by the life of worship lived out in all aspects of congregational life.

Martin correctly states, "Compartmentalization in ecclesial life ineluctably leads to fragmentation in the church's ministries and territorial divisiveness among the leadership. We need ways of conceiving the church that reveal its organic unity and yet acknowledge the marvelous plurality within it."[10] Effective planning must follow this important principle of relational integration of learning in the congregation's education programming.

Children need intergenerational experiences for their spiritual formation. Separating them from the congregation at worship and segregating them in church programs that exclude them from the larger life of the congregation is a spiritual disservice to them. Children and youth hear lip service given to the idea that they are an important part of the church, but their experiences teach them differently. When denied full participation, children and youth lose educational values inherent in being a part of the larger community of faith and the communal formation that is necessary for faith development. Dean Blevins contends, "Persons are shaped into Christian character and transformed doxologically as they participate faithfully (i.e., intentionally) in the discrete practices that identify the life of the faith community."[11]

A grandmother approached me after a Wednesday evening church meal. She had started bringing her two grandsons to church on Wednesday evenings for the meal and educational activities. She expressed concern that her grandchildren were overhearing prayer requests at the start of the meals related to some scary things: illnesses, accidents, hospitalization, cancer, anxieties, and deaths. I agreed with her that those were scary things, but that she was missing something else that was happening. Her grandchildren were witnessing how members of a community of faith share their anxieties and worries with one another. Her grandchildren were learning how members of a church had a place to share their concerns openly and how they prayed for one another. They were learning that it was unnecessary to keep scary things to themselves, because the faith community is a safe place to share those fears. They were learning that even adults had fears, but that they trusted those fears to God through prayer and found support from their church. I pointed out that her grandchildren were also overhearing some good things people were sharing—answers to prayers, celebrations, and expressions of love for one another. It was quite dramatic to see the "Aha!" moment she experienced as she realized that her grandchildren were really learning how a community of faith works.

We are, and become, what we do. Children who are encouraged to participate in the act of giving an offering during corporate worship learn that giving is a communal responsibility and not just a personal matter. Our theology shapes our practices, and our practices shape our faith. The patterns and practices of our community of faith become a mutual way of life. To be Christian is to be a part of the body of Christ and to participate fully in the church—conforming to, and being formed into, the likeness of Christ. Daniel Ciobotea reminds us, "The book of Acts underlines very clearly the importance of the gathered community as a place of spiritual formation and theological experience, since the Holy Spirit descends on the community which is persevering in prayer 'with one mind,' while the disciples are 'all together in one place' (Acts 2:1)."[12]

## Conclusion

The community-of-faith approach to Christian education formation is communal in nature and appreciates that relationships in the context of a congregation mediate Christian formation. The congregation is a community of faith. This construct is vital to understanding how a church needs to plan its education ministry. Intergenerational experiences, experiential learning, worship, and reflection, to mention just a few, are essential education practices of the communal nature of congregational life. In the next chapters we turn our attention to these and other principles of this particular approach to Christian education formation, one that acknowledges that, because a local congregation is a community of faith, it requires a planning process that is sensitive to how faith is formed in a communal context.

# 2

# The Congregation as Community of Faith

Occasionally, enthusiastic, but often dissatisfied, church educators call us to create within their congregations a model of seminary or "school for faith." They earnestly desire to make Christian education and learning a more serious enterprise in their congregation. These passionate educators want their church members to take learning as seriously as seminarians who wrestle with deep theological thoughts, engage in formative practices such as "critical theological reflection," and take the study of the biblical text seriously. They want to move Bible study in the church from a naïve devotional parochialism to a critical, and responsible, handling of the word of God.

Three congregations implemented this desire. One congregation created a "mini-seminary" for their youth program with short "courses" that parallel those of a basic seminary divinity degree. Another congregation is offering a course in New Testament Greek. A third congregation offers a lay institute program with a full schedule of academic classes modeled after an academy, with course fees, textbooks, exams, and certificates of achievement. (They "graduate" their students in a formal ceremony.)

Any attempt to take Christian education seriously in the congregation is a good thing, and we celebrate the rigorous administrative and educational processes. However, duplicating a schooling model in a congregational setting unsettles us. Ultimately, the ability to educate people in faith by borrowing instructional models and approaches to learning from another context (such as a school or the academy) is suspect. To put it bluntly, the passion and commitment to "real" education we applaud, but people cannot be "schooled" in faith.

Two facts work against "schooling" people in faith in the congregational setting: (1) instructional and didactic approaches do not fully address the nature of faith and how it is formed, and (2) the congregation, a religious organization, is by nature a *community of faith*, not a "school." Teaching and learning are critically important enterprises of the church. Still, its context dictates that *the ways* of teaching and learning need to be congruent to its nature. People need to "learn faith" in the ways faith is *actually* formed, and people need to learn in community via the ways that communities *actually* go about forming (educating) their members.

### What Makes a Congregation a Community of Faith?[1]

Congregational education leaders must approach their ministry, decision-making process, and program management with the understanding that a congregation is, at heart, more community than organization. The congregation's primary enterprise is the shaping of the faith of its members and of those to whom it reaches out in witness and ministry. Diana Butler Bass explains, "The primary job of the church is to be a spiritual community that forms people in faith."[2]

The way congregations go about doing that is primarily through the shared communal practices that flow out of a congregation's culture, not by programmatic means. Formal programs have an appropriate place. Programs are the means through which we enable communal relationships to be cultivated, perpetuated, and institutionalized. Our problem comes when we make programs primary over community relationships and those practices that cultivate faith.

The pastor and staff of Central Community Church consulted with me about their education programming.[3] This congregation had experienced rapid growth over the past six years. In response to the growth in numbers—with varied population groups of families, children, youth, and adults—this congregation had quickly added staff members to address ministry and education programming needs (sometimes adding two pastoral program staff persons in one year!). Just when they thought they had "everyone in place," they found themselves stuck. Programs did not take off. Church members were not participating as expected in many of the new educational opportunities the staff initiated. Programs created to meet the needs of members were met with lukewarm responses.

After much conversation, an assessment of their education programs, and an examination of the dynamics of their congregation's practices, the problem became apparent to the pastor and staff. They suffered from the uncritical proliferation of programs. In an enthusiastic attempt to address numerical growth, they had created one program after another with little attention to how those programs would impact life together in the community. The intelligent, well-intentioned staff created good programs. They erred in over-focusing on programs while failing to respect the dynamics at the heart of their congregation–the ways communities develop and settle into meaningful ways of practicing life together. Ironically, an uncritical approach to planning results in further fragmentation of the community of faith–working against the church's nature as an expression of genuine Christian community. As Robert O'Gorman wrote, "The crucial service of the parish today is to generate and develop community life in a society where fragmentation is the norm."[4]

Congregations are not just communities, but *communities of faith.* They center life together on rituals of meaning (such as worship, fellowships, and eating together), through conversations about belief and values (in formal education events and programs, or through casual conversations), and by the confession of a shared faith (through formal and informal worship experiences). As in all communities, practices and values in congregations are negotiated, shared, modified over time, and inculcated into the lives of the participants.

The reasons individuals join a congregation are varied. The most common reasons have everything to do with meeting the needs–whether actual or perceived–people believe can be found only through the shared, corporate religious experiences a congregation (as a faith community) offers. People look to their "church community" for: affirmation of their beliefs or guidance in forming beliefs, the opportunity to participate in meaningful practices, getting help in rearing children in faith, worshiping together in meaningful ways, finding friendships and support, having a sense of the holy in both place and experience, and having a sense of belonging. Congregations are genuine faith communities because they are places where people come together to participate in, and practice, the shared religious values that inform both corporate and individual identity. Two key components that facilitate the formation and sustaining of community are shared language and being together.

## Shared Language

In a faith community, language serves a formative function and is one indicator that a congregation is a genuine community of faith. That is, the community's idiom–consisting of its vocabulary, patterns of speech, spoken rituals and rites (such as greetings, blessings, and prayers)–functions in ways that shape the faith of its members. For idiom to be formative, the language a local congregation uses must have two components: (1) it must be grounded in the shared cultural experiences of its members; and (2) it must remain sufficiently *religiously* distinctive so as to express the community's peculiar identity and its adherence to a faith tradition.

The shared experiences of the congregation may include part of the language of a larger denomination or faith tradition; more important, however, they must also include the localized story of the particular faith tradition and history of the community. The local stories that arise out of the members' shared experiences are what carry their interpretation of the meaning of God's activity in the life of the community and of its members. Furthermore, these stories are localized because they are told in the idiom of the local congregation. Giving attention to and shaping its own language is one of the primary ways that a congregation acquires an identity.

Creating opportunities for congregational members to do this by "telling our story" must be both valued and implemented as a critical education function. Congregational leaders must program and schedule regular and frequent opportunities for the community members to hear and tell their stories of interpretive meaning. In chapter 6 we will examine how using the Christian Church Year as a framework for planning the Christian education formation program can help in this regard.

The distinctiveness of your congregation's communal language is also essential for the faith formation of its members. Uncritical attempts to borrow language from popular culture or from another tradition, ungrounded in shared religious experiences, in an attempt to "accommodate" seekers or potential members may prove to have the opposite effect. Imposing such language on the faith community serves only to deny the distinctive identity of your congregation. Further, the power of language leaves open the temptation to adopt the values that the borrowed language conveys–some of which may be foreign, or even antagonistic, to your congregation's values.

## Being Together

A second indication a congregation is a real community is that it facilitates ways for its members to be together. Congregations provide spaces and places to participate in activities, programs, and events that allow people to spend time together doing things they find meaningful. The huge investments that congregations make in buildings and campuses are not just institutional symbols of power or affluence; they also shape how people live out their faith and relate to each other in community. In the same way, formal programs, regardless of their announced agenda (for instance, worship, learning, mission activities, administration, or business), help fulfill the congregation's members' need to spend time together in shared experiences.

The dilemma contemporary American congregations face, however, is the tension between the separateness and togetherness forces that dominate the culture. People yearn for and seek out groups that will make them feel at home in a complex and confusing world. At the same time, they resist any group that makes demands or attempts to impose ethical norms or makes prophetic calls to accountability. Congregants will welcome messages of affirmation and inspiration and will assent to general biblically prophetic statements about ethical living. But any attempt to directly challenge individual lifestyle choices or personal practices and habits will not be easily tolerated. In those instances one is likely to hear, "Pastor, you've gone from preachin' to meddlin'!" Congregations live in this cultural tension and spend a lot of time attempting to be genuine communities of faith while juggling these contradictory forces of togetherness and separateness, acceptance and accountability.

As a result, congregations are tempted to "define community down" as they organize themselves as religious institutions. Some narrow the scope of who belongs in the community by overtly inviting people who are alike in some way, such as those of a particular ethnicity, or socioeconomic level, or similar educational background. Other congregations stress a "community-as-support-group" approach, expecting their members to develop close interpersonal relationships in an atmosphere of emotional support and mutual encouragement. In terms of education programming the temptation is to try to create events and programs for "niche" groups or populations through which the needs and interests of the focus group become paramount, or, typically, organizing the education program as separate "schools" for children, youth, and adults. The danger here is that this over-focus on providing for the exclusive needs and interests of "niche" groups within the congregation only ensures that they will be disconnected from the practices and culture of the larger community of faith and therefore fail to "be community together."

Being together in community involves more than a focus on people's needs. Community implies mutuality. In this sense faith communities, with their religious traditions, offer a truer image: community as a gathering that enlarges, challenges, and completes the individual's life of faith by providing a place where both strengths and needs are welcomed in the body of Christ. A community is more than another name for intimate self-disclosure and emotional support. A community creates opportunities for being together where the possibilities of shared values can move members to action in the public square, undertaken in a context of mutual commitment and inspired by a corporate vision of the Church's mission in the world. In other words, the reasons certain programs and opportunities for meeting and working together are created—and others are not—have to do with the corporate values that are important to *all* of the members of the church.

That does not mean that everyone needs to attend everything the church offers, but all the members agree that these programs and events are "the things we do." This, in part, was the situation with which the pastor and staff of Central Community Church were struggling. Despite a proliferation of programs designed to meet the needs and interests of particular groups within the church, they were not addressing the culture, values, and norms of the church community as a whole. As the congregation experienced fast numerical growth, they had difficulty shifting from being "church together" to participating in church in more narrowly focused, age-graded, interest-oriented groups.

Creating a shared life together requires that congregational leaders address fundamental questions about the congregation as community. During the course of a congregation's lifespan and development, these fundamental questions in relation to its education formation planning need to be revisited often.[5]

- What is the major purpose of this group? How does it relate to the mission and current vision of the congregation?
- How fully are members involved in the life of the church community? What level of commitment in time, resource, and participation does our programming facilitate? Inhibit?

- In what ways is intimacy, honesty, and mutual accountability encouraged?
- Is the leadership function for educational programming shared, or is it delegated to one person or position?
- In what ways is the community effective in teaching, sharing, and perpetuating its values and beliefs through its programming?
- In what ways are group behavior and norms regulated? Is each programmed segment or event consistent with the church's corporate values and identity?
- In what ways are group members evaluated as to their Christian discipleship, growth, and level of participation?
- How effective is the community in inviting and assimilating new members into existing programs and communal events and practices?
- What does it mean to belong to this community? How does it happen? What is assumed and expected of the members?

These questions hint at the ways the congregation functions as a community beneath the surface of program titles and schedules. Because each congregation is unique, each must answer those questions for itself. Fayette Veverka wrote:

> While participating in the larger Christian tradition, a congregation develops its own distinctive sense of identity and mission through the interaction of its members in response to the situations they find themselves in. This "corporate personality" is shaped by the particular history, social location, structure, membership, size, and beliefs of the faith community and has a perduring [very durable] power that is not easily changed.[6]

Planning a program of education formation for a congregation requires that we give attention to the uniqueness of our community of faith to ensure integrity and congruence between who we are and what we do in the formation of our members. If congregational leaders are unable to answer these questions about the congregation's education formation planning, they will also lack understanding about how well their congregation is functioning as an authentic Christian community.

The congregation, as a church, is a local body of believers whose religious hope is expressed in their life together and in their ministries of service, learning, and worship. Because the mission of a congregation includes both internal and external ends (a movement inward and a movement outward), the church must organize, plan, and develop the social forms of a faith community, and no less so in its education formation programming. Faith communities, including congregations, must find and nourish ways to express the communion that exists among their members, from the shared meaning and identity that make them distinctive groups, to participation in the common mission that moves their members into the world. Ultimately, a congregation's mission is that of the Church: to witness to the world the redemptive presence of God among us. No greater vehicle exists for that witness than a community of faith.

### The Need for a Different Approach to Christian Education

Shifting our understanding of Christian education toward formation in a faith community context calls for a shift in our education approach. Theological educators have been calling for a more authentic, meaningful, corporate, and communal way of doing Christian education in the congregational setting for decades. The social dimension of education is a fundamental concept in education philosophies. Elizabeth Potter claimed, "Any adequate epistemology must account for knowledge in social terms. Whatever else we may wish to say about knowledge, we must recognize that it is a social affair."[7]

Wanda Stahl stated the case bluntly: "Individualistic epistemologies have unconsciously shaped much of our ministry and education without adequate analysis of whether they are consistent with Christian beliefs or effective in Christian formation.... Our cultural milieu of individualism has blinded us to the limits it places on Christian formation and ministry."[8]

Shifting our approach to planning and organizing the congregation's Christian education formation ministry toward a more communal frame of reference will not be easy. It requires us to redefine what it means to educate our members in faith. It means we will have to redefine our assumptions about basic components of our education enterprise, such as the role of the teacher, clarity about what constitutes "learning," and what the curriculum is.

### Church Life as Curriculum[9]

Shifting the education paradigm in a congregation toward a faith community approach will redefine our concept about curriculum. Whenever I get a call from church educators–clergy or lay–asking about a curricular resource for their church, inevitably they are asking for a teaching resource product or published curriculum. I redirect them toward answering certain questions about their congregation: questions about the type of education programs the church offers, the leadership in those programs, the makeup of their membership, and the size and location of their congregation. Those questions they answer easily. Then I ask questions about their congregation's culture, its values, its educational formation goals, and its philosophy of education. That's when I get thundering silence at the other end of the phone.

It's hard to recommend a curricular resource without understanding the nature of a faith community. To be effective, any curricular product must be congruent with a congregation's culture, values, practices, identity, and goals. *Those very things constitute a congregation's real curriculum.* Maria Harris identified the total life of the congregation as the primary religious education curriculum of any congregation. Her work frames a congregation's "course of the church's life" through the practices of teaching (*didachè*), worship (*leitourgia*), community (*koinonia*), proclamation (*kerygma*), and service or outreach (*diakonia*).[10]

Redefining our understanding of curriculum as consisting primarily of the experience of the life of the church shifts our whole framework for Christian education. The congregation's real curriculum is "all those relationships and experiences which are offered to individuals and groups as they participate actively in the life of a congregation."[11] Adopting this perspective for planning the Christian education formation programs in the church offers significant advantages over other approaches:

- It allows Christian teaching to be informed by the life structure of your church.
- It allows Christian teaching and learning to flow from your church's core identity.
- It taps into the rich tradition of the seasons and cycles of the Christian Church Year.
- It offers limitless possibilities for structuring Christian teaching through the year.
- It helps make for a more natural planning approach to Christian teaching and learning.
- It helps integrate the activities of teaching and learning into the ongoing, cyclical life of the church.
- It helps guard against uncritical proliferation of programs.

- It makes the creation of your own unique curriculum more feasible.

The concept of church life as curriculum takes into account that curriculum is much more than the literature that we choose to use in Sunday morning classes and in study groups. A congregation that relies heavily on purchased mass-produced literature and teaching resources becomes dependent on a product produced by someone who does not know anything about the uniqueness of their church's life. The learner or teacher who relies too heavily on purchased educational literature may base his or her understanding of the faith more on what a stranger thinks than on what his or her church believes and practices.

Publishing houses do good service for our churches, but they don't write curriculum for your congregation. They write curricula to sell to as many churches as are required to make that endeavor a feasible business venture! This is not to discount the quality and validity of curriculum publishers and their ministries. They are conscientious in trying to supply much-needed resources to churches. But they can't tailor-make for your congregation the specific curricular resource it needs for its particular epoch of communal development, its cultural setting, its communal issues, or its unique population. This truth puts a new light on the need for the design, use, and application of curricula in more authentic ways in our local churches.

We said that the church's real curriculum is "all those relationships and experiences which are offered to individuals and groups as they participate actively in the life of a congregation." Let's examine the components of this new definition of curriculum and explore some of its implications.

### All Those Relationships...

If one truth separates Christian teaching from other forms of education, it is that Christian teaching is relational and communal. At heart Christian education formation is not about a creed, or a book, or body of knowledge, but a person: Jesus Christ. Christian formation is a product of being in relationship with Christ in the context of the community of faith: the Church.

The only authentically human thing we can do with persons is to be in relationship with them. It's easy to lose sight of that essential truth when educational programming starts focusing on concepts, issues, techniques, methodologies, programs, technologies, or on meeting institutional rather than personal needs. For example, churches often feel a need to incorporate the latest in high-tech teaching equipment (videos, computers, "Christian" video games) if they are to succeed in teaching today's learners. If authentic Christian education formation involves the use of "Christian" methodologies, then high-tech equipment may be the worst thing one can introduce into the church learning environment. While we may be tempted to compete with what the community schools have to offer by way of instructional technology, we need to remember that, since the nature of Christian education formation is in essence a relational dynamic that happens in the context of a community of faith, it is inappropriate to compete with schooling methods that are essentially instructional.

Communal formative relationships do not translate through video, computer, or hi-tech visuals. Relationship happens person to person; it always has and always will. Hi-tech methods may help or enhance the instructional process, but they can never substitute or make a significant impact on the kind of formative relationships that take place in the corporate dimensions of learning in Christian community: being and growing spiritually in relationship with God, self, and others. Faith formation depends on the epistemology of relationships. Simply put, relationships mediate spiritual formation.

If Christian education is to be authentic, then the methods we use in teaching and learning will not be didactic ones, but those of a communal relational nature. The phrase "all those relationships" hints at the significance and place of community in curriculum. Segmented groupings of age-grading, narrowly focused programs, and classes will always be secondary to the power, character, and dynamics of learning within the community at large.

### And Experiences...

Christian educators have long confessed to the detrimental effects of our Western emphasis on cerebral faith. At its worst, a content or concepts-focused Christian education codifies our beliefs to a manageable cognitive exercise of "right belief" at the expense of those other important dimensions of our person: our emotions and will. This often tends to give rise to an adolescent posture that to know the "right answers" about the Christian life is tantamount to having lived them!

God is living, personal, and relational. God cannot be contained in mere concepts, ideas, or doctrines. In the depth of the spiritual life the goal is not to comprehend God, but to be in communion with God. If Christian education is to be authentic, then the total person must experience the learning of faith mentally, emotionally, volitionally, and spiritually. Learning will cease to be exclusively an exercise of the mind. It will become the experience of living the life of God in us and among us in its fullest expression according to Jesus' intent: "I am one with them, and you are one with me, so that they may become completely one. Then this world's people will know that you sent me. They will know that you love my followers as much as you love me" (Jn. 17:23 CEV). It does not take a huge stretch of the imagination to realize that planning for Christian education formation will require a greater emphasis on experiential learning. The good news is that the experiences needed to facilitate this kind of learning are a resource readily available in the congregational community through its religious and communal practices. As we will see later, the way people learn the practices of community is by direct participation in the practices themselves. You learn to do what you *do* and not something else. As the bromide teaches: practice makes perfect. We learn through our actions, not through our listening or our test scores. Daily deeds form lifetime habits.

## Offered to Individuals and Groups...

Church life as curriculum helps situate the focus of Christian education experiences in the context of congregational life–the faith community. Individuals and groups are understood as persons who have, in one way or another, at some level joined with a particular community of faith in significant levels of commitment. The curricula that are offered to individuals and groups flow out of the practice of life together in the community of faith. The educational formation practices that constitute the church life curriculum are offered with the intent of helping to move individuals toward the center of the life of the community. Moving toward the center of community life means greater commitment and investment of self in Christian living in and through the life of the church.

If Christian teaching is to be authentic, then the curricula offered to individuals and groups within the church must have common overarching goals consistent with the core values and identity of the community. All curricula, for example, will include helping individuals enter into a personal relationship with Jesus Christ, move them toward affirming the binding covenant of the faith community, then challenge and enable them to live out the intent and calling expressed in that covenant.

## As They Participate Actively...

Learning for faith formation is not a passive activity. Formation is an experience that brings about change in a person's behavior, attitudes, and values. Learning in, and through, formative relationships calls for active participation in the lives of others within the church community and in the world. If Christian teaching is to be authentic, then it must call learners and teachers to go about their learning, not in the laboratory of a classroom or school, but in the arena of life and living. This praxis approach to Christian faith formation challenges us to make a greater effort toward education by discipleship. Successful learning in the Christian life happens in the living and doing, and so curriculum moves out of classrooms and fellowship halls and worship rooms, and into the experience of life together and in the realm of daily living.

## In the Life of a Congregation...

At odds with popular cultural notions of individualism, the Christian life can be lived only in community. The church is the community that safeguards, calls forth, commissions, equips, and holds accountable her members. The way a church chooses to structure its living out the calling of God reflects what its members value. What is celebrated? What is ignored? Where are most of their energies invested? What is talked about? Who is invited into and sought out for the community? Who is excluded by intent or neglect? On what does the church spend its money? In what proportions? For what purposes is time allotted? For what is space made available?

The course of the life of the church is a "relational curriculum" that influences and shapes our faith. Christian maturity is not defined by independence, but by inter-dependence—the need and willingness to be in relationship with one another, to depend on each other, and to work collaboratively to make meaning of our experiences. Roberta Gilbert wrote, "In the realm of the purely personal, after food, water, and shelter—the quality of relationships most often determines the quality of life."[12] The same is true of congregational life. As we experience life together in community, two important results occur: (1) Our faith is influenced and shaped by other believers, and (2) we complement one another and, thus, fulfill our corporate calling.

If Christian education formation is to be authentic, then it must flow out of and reflect the life of the congregation. To be effective, Christian education cannot be an afterthought. Christian education formation cannot be delegated to a status of secondary importance to the life of the congregation or its members; rather, it needs to be valued and central to the life of the community—integral, highly visible, supported, and celebrated.

## The Power of Christian Education Formation in the Faith Community

We are advocating a particular way of thinking about congregations, as genuine communities of faith, which calls for a particular approach to planning for Christian education in the congregational setting. The enterprise for educating in faith in that setting is unique. The church is not a school; it is a bona fide community of faith. Therefore, its ways of educating in faith must be congruent to its nature. Knowledge and faith are located in the concrete and particular—in the practices of faith that constitute life together in community. Learning about faith occurs in the practice of faith.

A unique part of the nature of Christian faith development is that it happens in community through formation in communal relationships. Planning for Christian education formation must encourage a commitment to the common good as essential to community identity. This contrasts with ways of planning Christian education that over-focus on the individual needs or predilections of individuals who stand apart from life in community. The faith community approach to Christian formation education will build and reinforce integration of the corporate church body, but also of individuals who will be able to see themselves as part of that body. By using the Christian Church Year framework, as we will see in chapter 6, we can foster an integration of the local congregation's identity with that of the larger Church.

The community of faith approach to planning and educating the members of a congregation in faith requires collaboration and team leadership. We will recommend a model for an education leadership team in chapter 3. Changing long-established ways of planning for, and the practice of, education is not easy; it requires time and work. No new model, however appropriate, is a quick fix. Churches that are serious about education ministry will recognize the values that team leadership provides for planning effective faith formation. A primary value that lies at the heart of this particular planning approach is that education planning is a holistic practice. In other words, effective education planning addresses the way persons of all ages are educated in faith in all contexts of congregational life, how all aspects of congregational life work together toward that end, and how a relationship with God and others is formed in and through community. This means effective education planning requires a leadership team that focuses on all aspects of congregational life, rather than on a particular segment of church life. An education leadership team that gives oversight to the entire education ministry of the church is indispensable to congregations that view the church as a faith community.

## Conclusion

We are challenging your congregation to consider a new way of being and doing Christian education based on the understanding that the church is a community of faith and that a new approach to planning is necessary to effectively educate persons in faith in that context. We are calling your church leaders to engage in a discussion about, and practice of, education planning that is relational and corporate. The community-of-faith approach to Christian education formation helps create and sustain an ecology of formation education in the community of faith—a holistic, integrated, and interdependent network of mutually sustaining relationships. This new holistic ecology will require a focus on the communal over the individualistic; a move from an exclusively cognitive emphasis to a relational epistemology; a move from programmatic to cultural contexts for learning; a shift from predominantly didactic and schooling approaches to tapping into the power of community formation; and a shift from a curriculum for beliefs toward a curriculum for faith formation.

# PART II: Organization for Planning

*The Practical Structure of a*
*Christian Faith Community*

# 3

# Organizing the Christian Education Leadership Team

We miss many of the television shows of the past. *Andy Griffith Show, Lassie, Leave it to Beaver,* and a talking horse named *Mister Ed* were some of our favorites. Another we enjoyed was *The Lone Ranger,* set in the time of the Western frontier days. The Lone Ranger, after being wounded in an ambush, was befriended by a Native American named Tonto. The title *Kemosabe* ("faithful friend" or "trusty scout") rings in our ears as we think back on these television episodes, along with the words, "A fiery horse with the speed of light, a cloud of dust, and a hearty, 'Hi-yo, Silver, away!'" The Lone Ranger and Tonto, with their trusted horses Silver and Scout, led the fight for law and order.

In the fight for justice, the Lone Ranger often took things into his own hands, making decisions outside of the established system of law and order. That's probably where we get the often-used phrase in church life, "We have a lot of Lone Rangers around here." The implication is that some individuals or small groups of people in church make decisions on their own without working with others and without going through proper decision-making channels. It happens all the time. And it is a recipe for misunderstanding and mistrust that often leads to conflict.

Communal congregational life cannot be healthy and effective when one, two, or a few people run the show with agendas that do not consider the overall life of the congregation. Congregations need an effective education leadership team whose responsibility is to plan, coordinate, and oversee the education life of the congregation.

## The Advantages of a Leadership Team

Doing education program planning through a central leadership team has distinct advantages. The faith community approach to education planning works best with a primary education team that gives oversight to all educational aspects of congregational life. This central coordinating team structure helps ensure that the church education ministries are programmed for integration and balance, with a view toward meeting the educational needs of the congregation as a whole. The team helps avoid fragmentation and competition for resources that often develop when individuals or narrowly focused groups have responsibility for particular ministry areas. Additional teams will become necessary as a congregation becomes larger and the education ministry grows more complex. But the function of education leadership for a community of faith is best attained when the entire scope of congregational life is addressed by a leadership team assigned that purpose.

Medium-sized congregations (150 to 300 average worship attendance) commonly give over education program planning and oversight to a single congregational staff member. Too often those staff persons work in isolation and typically have responsibility for multiple areas of ministry programming.[1] For example, many congregations support their education staffing needs with persons who have combination positions—music and youth; education and administration; children and family life; etc. One of two scenarios often happens. In one, any existing education planning group will likely disband when the new staff person arrives, happily giving over leadership and oversight to a program they've struggled to make work. Or, in the other, with no existing team or committee in place, the new program ministry staff person neglects to recruit, train, and develop a leadership team and winds up working as the Lone Ranger in the program areas assigned. It does not take long before ministry programs are seen as "belonging" to the staff person, created in his or her image. It won't take long to burn out the staff member who must bear the burden of carrying out multiple ministry responsibilities that grow more complex and demanding with each year.

Many congregations use an exclusively age-graded programming approach for education leadership.[2] These churches may develop separate age-graded leadership teams or committees and give them the responsibility for planning and carrying out ministry for a particular age group. For example, many congregations have a children's leadership team, a youth leadership group, and, perhaps, an adult education committee. More often than not, however, the education programming for the church will fall on a paid professional or volunteer staff person who gives vision and oversight to these ministry areas, but who often tends to work in isolation.

This is problematic for several reasons. First, it sets the congregation up for a fragmented education program. Second, it works against the nature of the church. As previously stated, the church is a faith community, not a school made up of departments with specialized topics of study or particularized populations. Any approach to planning that segregates the leadership and planning process of the community of faith is not supportive of, or congruent with, the inherent communal nature of the church. Effective planning requires systemic integration.

Education planning must be congruent with the ends desired, because process determines outcome. If our desire is to educate in faith for the formation of a community of faith, then we must plan in ways that will facilitate holistic integration of learning in the corporate body. An approach to leadership that does not use an education leadership team to plan and guide all aspects of faith life cannot successfully meet the educational needs of a community of faith in a holistic way. The practice of using separate and isolated age-graded or group-focused leadership teams works against a congregation's attempts to educate persons in faith as a community of faith. The following examples will highlight that truth:

- Isolated age-graded leadership groups often end up in turf wars. They compete with one another for resources and calendar time. Persons on these teams often develop tunnel vision. They become so focused on *their* area of ministry and *their* population that they fail to perceive and address the broader educational needs of the congregation. For example, they may fail to appreciate the need for intergenerational experiences in a faith community. All persons, regardless of age, are influenced for faith formation by all participants in the congregation.
- Isolated age-graded education leadership groups often result in a "Lone Ranger" planning mentality. They make their plans without consideration of other groups. This lack of

communication and integration may lead to church member conflicts and a conflict of goals. Ultimately, this may lead to rifts and a lack of a sense of accountability among groups and individuals who are supposed to be involved in the same enterprise: the education of the members into the unity of the body of Christ.

- Isolated age-graded planning groups can wield more influence and power than other leadership teams if the members of the team are stronger personalities, more energetic, or more willful than the leaders of other age-graded teams. This results in a lack of balance in education planning. When some teams appear to receive more attention, more funding, and calendaring priority, only frustration follows. It is not uncommon for the populations who tend to be the focus of parental anxiety—children and teenagers—to receive the most programmatic support, have the loudest advocates, and absorb an inordinate amount of resources when no voice exists for balance and no forum for integration.

A lack of commitment to the welfare of the whole makes it extremely difficult to bring isolated age-graded planning groups together for communication and collaborative planning. This lack of commitment to the corporate body leads to frustration in leaders who desire to collaborate with others. Simply stated, the isolated age-graded approach to education leadership is difficult to manage and does not adequately address the educational needs of the faith community as a body.

One additional potential liability is that isolated age-graded leadership planning groups can have an adverse influence on relationship building, collaboration, and communication among the leaders responsible for planning the education ministries of the congregation. Worse, leaving age-graded program planning to a single staff person (or an individual paid professional or volunteer), who works in burdened isolation and who is left to his or her own resources, places great limitations on effective program planning. This is not to suggest that age-graded programs are not appropriate in congregational life. What we are suggesting is that a planning approach that uses one integrated education leadership team to give oversight to the education life of the congregation, rather than isolated age-graded leadership teams, is a more effective, and efficient, way to work.

## The "Christian Education Leadership Team" Approach: Why It Works

Administering a comprehensive education program is a complex enterprise. An education leadership team approach makes the numerous leadership functions of an integrated and comprehensive Christian education formation program manageable. Using a "Christian Education Leadership Team" to plan and give oversight to the Christian education ministry of the congregation is the most effective way to carry out these varied leadership functions. First of all, working together as an education planning team prevents competition for limited resources by age-graded education ministry areas. The team is empowered by the congregation to plan and make decisions regarding the integrated corporate education life of the congregation. In the planning process the team members coordinate resources of budget, volunteers, building space, and scheduling rather than competing for them. This eliminates potential territorial issues related to programs. When one education ministry dominates programming, all ministry areas lose. A well-coordinated and cooperating "Christian Education Leadership Team" (hereafter CELT) will value all ministries as deserving of attention and development and will strive for balance as appropriate.

Second, the team structure facilitates the members' ability to value the corporate identity of the congregation and to maintain its sense of community. By working together to design a holistic and integrated education program, the corporate identity and values of the community (rather than personal predilections or force of personality) become interwoven into the life of the congregation.

### Getting the Right People on the Team: Calling and Gifts

Your CELT will be effective to the degree that it is comprised of members whose gifts match the functional needs of the team. Congregations too often enlist leaders without giving consideration to the functional needs of the team or the gifts of the members who are asked to be a part of the team. This practice can hinder the CELT from carrying out its work of planning, coordinating, and evaluating.

If we consider the gifts and skills, passions, and personalities of persons before enlisting them for service, we will form a more effective CELT. The effectiveness of the team is directly related to the gifts and skill sets of the team members, and their freedom to live out their calling in obedience to God by using their gifts as they support the work of the team in building up the body of Christ.

Another significant consideration must be addressed. We must be clear about the functions we ask persons to carry out. One mistake we often make is enlisting leaders and team or committee members based on their passions rather than their gifts. For example, the chairperson of the CELT should not be enlisted solely on the basis of that person's passion for education! Passion for the ministry is important, but it isn't sufficient in itself for effectiveness. What is essential is that person's ability to carry out the function of group leadership. The CELT will not be effective if the chairperson does not possess the gift and skill set for leadership. This point cannot be stressed enough. Church leadership teams' seats often are filled by persons who occupy a slot on the team for many reasons, but not for the right reasons. People *should* be included on the team only if they possess gifts that match the functional needs of the team. It is critical, then, to have a clear understanding of the task of the CELT so that persons with the right gifts may be enlisted for service. Simply stated, we need to be clear about the functions we are asking persons to consider. Many committee and team-related problems would subside if congregations understood and practiced this leadership principle.

The chairperson of the CELT is called to a leadership task that differs from the functions asked of the other team members. The chairperson must be a person who can lead an effective meeting and guide a team in collaborative work. The leadership responsibility of the chairperson requires effectiveness in carrying out the following functions: setting an agenda, facilitating discussion, keeping team members on track, dealing with team members who are excessively talkative or opinionated, managing conflict, setting goals, determining action plans, engaging all team members in the work of the team, seeing that team members receive adequate training, fostering imagination, following up on tasks, assessing the work of the team, and leading the team to address the educational needs of the congregation.

In addition to being gifted for leadership in their particular areas of responsibility, members of the CELT need to be persons who

- are familiar with and have an appreciation for the history and tradition of the congregation;
- are aligned with the congregation's identity and mission;
- are supporters of the church and participate in the diverse experiences of congregational life;
- are supportive of the clergy staff;
- are able to understand and articulate the church's education philosophy;

- are learners who are committed to personal growth;
- are good thinkers who are able to reason theologically, brainstorm, weigh options, compromise for the common good, and make sound decisions;
- are able to work well with others;
- are effective at carrying out assigned tasks;
- are trusted and respected by the congregation;
- are able to commit the time and energy required of the work;
- are not encumbered with a specific agenda or have an axe to grind.

Members of the CELT should be among the best leaders of the congregation because their work impacts all aspects of congregational life.

### The Christian Education Leadership Team Structure

The Christian Education Leadership Team should consist of at least the following positions:

**The Chairperson.** This person functions as coordinator and group facilitator. It is not necessary that this person be "an educator," since the function of the chairperson is to run an effective meeting and help the team do its work. If the CELT is a standing committee in the congregation's organizational structure, the chairperson may be an elected position with a specified rotation tenure (typically a three-year term). The chairperson typically sits on the chief coordinating leadership group in the church, such as a Church Council.

**The Co-chair.** This person will assist the chairperson and will preside over the team when the chair is absent. A wise practice is to let the co-chair assume the retiring chairperson's seat. This way you have a person-in-training for the position of chairperson. The co-chair will serve as recorder for the group meetings and will be assigned supportive administrative duties. For example, the co-chair records and distributes the minutes of the meetings and follows up with assignments such as making room reservations for events or making reservations with the childcare team or committee for an education event as needed. The co-chair may serve on the Church Council or the coordinating body.

**The Preschool Ministry Coordinator.** This person oversees and coordinates the preschool ministries and programs of the church. He or she works in conjunction with the CELT to plan, coordinate, and assess the preschool ministries of the congregation. The Preschool

Ministry Coordinator works with the Sunday School Coordinator to recruit teachers and helpers for the preschool Sunday School department. In larger congregations the coordinator will work closely with the professional staff person who oversees the preschool ministries. The coordinator then serves as a liaison between the staff person and the Christian Education Leadership Team.

**The Children's Ministry Coordinator.** This person oversees and coordinates the church's children's ministries and programs. He or she works in conjunction with the CELT to plan, coordinate, and assess the children's ministries of the congregation. The Children's Ministry Coordinator works with the Sunday School Coordinator to recruit teachers and helpers for the children's Sunday School department and classes. In a smaller congregation (50 to 150 members) you may combine the positions of Children and Preschool Ministries Coordinators. In larger congregations the coordinator will work closely with the professional staff person who oversees the children's ministries. The coordinator may then serve as a liaison between the staff person and the Christian Education Leadership Team.

**The Youth Ministry Coordinator.** This person oversees and coordinates the youth and student ministries and programs of the church. In larger churches, he or she works in conjunction with the church program staff person (the Minister of Youth or the Youth Pastor, for example) and with the CELT to plan, coordinate, and assess the youth ministries of the congregation. The Youth Ministry Coordinator works with the Sunday School Coordinator to recruit teachers and volunteers for the youth Sunday School department and classes. In larger congregations the coordinator will work closely with the professional staff person who oversees the youth ministries. The coordinator may then serve as a liaison between the staff person and the Christian Education Leadership Team.

**The Adult Ministry Coordinator.** This person oversees and coordinates the adult ministries and programs of the church. He or she works in conjunction with the church program staff person (the Minister of Education, the Pastor for Discipleship, Minister of Adult Education, or Minister of Spiritual Formation, for example) and with the CELT to plan, coordinate, and assess the adult ministries of the congregation. The Adult Ministry Coordinator works with the Sunday School Coordinator to recruit teachers and volunteers for the adult Sunday School department and classes. In larger congregations the coordinator will work closely with the professional staff person who oversees the adult ministries. The coordinator may then serve as a liaison between the staff person and the Christian Education Leadership Team.

**The Sunday School Coordinator.** This person oversees and coordinates the Sunday School or church school program in the church. He or she works in conjunction with the church program staff person (the Minister of Education, the Pastor for Discipleship, or Minister of Christian Formation, for example) and with the CELT to plan, coordinate, and assess the Sunday morning Bible study programs in the congregation. The Sunday School Coordinator works with the members of the CELT to recruit teachers and volunteers for the Sunday school.

**The Training Coordinator.** This person works with the CELT to assess the training needs in the congregation and to provide training events or programs as needed. For example, if the CELT determines a need for a new Sunday morning Bible study group and then recruits, with the Sunday School Coordinator, two new study leaders for that class, the Training Coordinator will provide for the training and orientation needs for those new group leaders. Or, when the CELT, along with the Children's Ministry Coordinator, selects the Vacation Bible School director, the Training Coordinator will work with that person to schedule and execute the training and orientation for the VBS program staff.

**A Staff Resource Person** (pastor, associate pastor, or staff). An important member of the CELT is the staff resource person. This person typically is a paid pastoral or program staff person such as a Director of Education, or a Minister of Education, or the staff person with primary responsibility for the formation education programs. This person serves as a resource for the CELT, but may also bear primary leadership responsibility for the CELT's effectiveness. However, the CELT does not exist to do the staff resource person's bidding. The responsibility for the church's education ministry belongs to the team members collectively. The function of the staff resource person is to help ensure that the CELT does its work effectively and to support, guide, encourage, and empower the CELT members to carry out their ministries. The staff resource person can provide theological leadership and expertise to the team by guiding discussions, providing resources, and interpreting the work of the team to the congregation. Since the staff resource person is connected to other key groups in the church, such as the pastoral staff and administrative leadership groups, he or she can help ensure integration between the work of the team and the global concerns of the congregation.

As your congregation's education programming needs grow and become more complex, you can add persons to the CELT to facilitate the work of planning, coordinating, and assessing. For example, if your congregation experiences a period with a large influx of new families with young children, you will naturally increase programming for both children and parents, and their families. During that time of program proliferation for families, childcare will become an issue. Don't expect parents of young children to show up for events at the church, or at a marriage enrichment retreat, if they have trouble finding childcare. In this case you will want to add a childcare coordinator. The Childcare Coordinator will work with the CELT to schedule childcare as needed for programs and events. He or she will have a budget line item under the Christian education portion of the

**Figure 3-1: The Basic Organization of the Christian Education Leadership Team**

**Figure 3-2: The Functions of the Christian Education Leadership Team**

Chairperson and Co-chair
(serve on Church Council)

Serve on the Church Council. Lead the Team

**The Christian Education Leadership Team**

*Planning
Coordinating
Assessing
Budgeting*

Sunday School Coordinator
Coordinates and directs the Sunday School

Staff Resource Person
Serves on the Church Council. Resources and supports the team

Training Coordinator
Coordinates and provides training for ministries

Youth Ministry Coordinator
Coordinates and directs the youth programs and events

Preschool Ministry Coordinator
Coordinates and directs the preschool programs and events

Adult Ministry Coordinator
Coordinates and directs the adult programs and events

Children's Ministry Coordinator
Coordinates and directs the children's programs and events

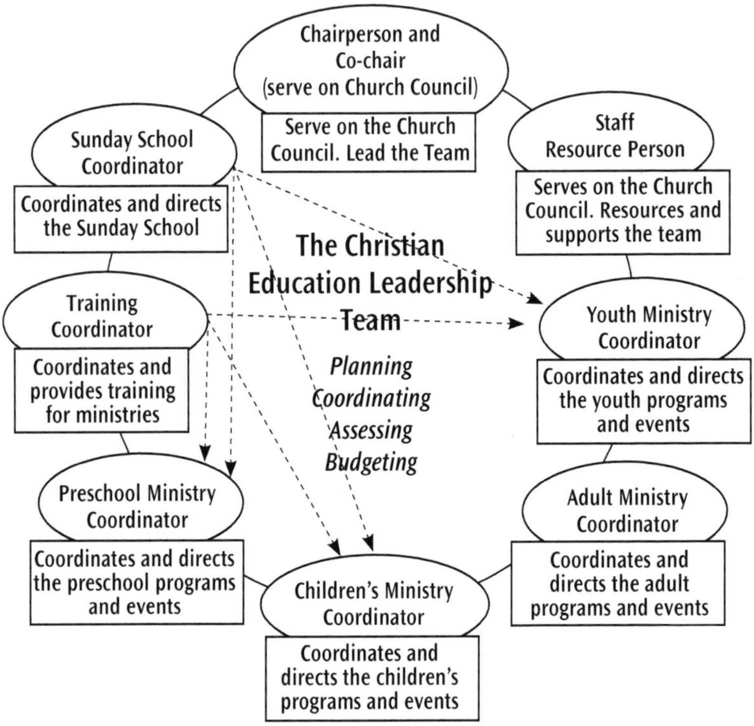

budget. Additionally, this coordinator will have the resource of the Training Coordinator to provide training and orientation to existing and new childcare providers and workers in the church to ensure quality, dependability, and compliance with any child protection policies established by the congregation.

Similarly, if your youth and student population increases (or when, in five to seven years, those children from the influx of new families have suddenly entered your youth department), you may need to add a person to oversee separate middle school and high school ministries, programs, and activities. In that event you keep the same structure with a youth ministries coordinator, but add two program area directors, one for middle school and one for high school (Or, divide the labor between the existing coordinator and one new person, each taking responsibility for one age-graded program area. See Figure 3-4 on page 42.) As the congregation grows numerically, and as the education programs develop, keep the same structure and the coordinating function of the CELT while adding persons to the organization as needed. Refer to the charts for examples of options related to the functions and size of your congregation.

### Figure 3-3: The Basic Organization of the Christian Education Leadership Team for a Small Congregation

*(Will work in congregations with up to 150 average worship attendance)*

### Training the Team

As educators who have served churches more than three decades, we have heard countless stories of experiences in other churches. We are continually surprised that most churches do not have well-functioning education teams that effectively guide the education ministries of the church. We are a bit less surprised that many church leadership teams are ineffective because they have not been adequately trained to carry out their work. Many churches give little attention to training. Churches that focus on the formation of leadership teams and the enlistment process without giving adequate attention to training needs will fail in their goal of providing effective leadership.

"That was a waste of time!" Many members express this sentiment when the team leader and team members have not been effectively trained in their work. Too often, one or two persons dominate the discussion and make decisions while most members sit idle with little to say. Some teams are content with one or two members doing most of the work while other members are not given anything to do. Many team members accept this state of affairs because they have not received training on how to be effective team members and because they are not held accountable. Chairpersons of leadership teams often have to feel their way blindly into the unknown because they receive little to no training on what it means to be an effective group

### Figure 3-4: The Basic Organization of the Christian Education Leadership Team for Larger Congregations

*(Will work in congregations with over 250 average worship attendance. Keep the basic structure but add persons as needed.)*

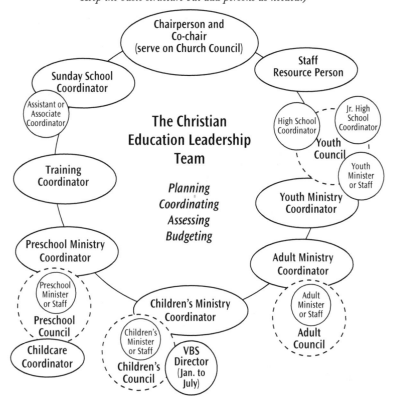

leader. At best, without proper training, leaders fall into the pattern of mimicking practices based on their past experiences—some good, and some poor.

Enlisting a CELT without giving proper attention to training will not result in effective planning. Team leaders and members need to be trained to carry out their functions and work together. A lack of understanding on the part of the chairperson and team members regarding the dynamics of effective teamwork will adversely affect the capacity of the team to plan effectively. Teams may go about their work with little consideration to their need for training until they get stuck, frustrated, and ultimately become ineffective. Sometimes, we place members on teams who have little interest or passion for the work they have been asked to do—and have no matching spiritual gifts to do the work. Passion and/or skills, however, cannot replace leadership capability when selecting leaders. A lack of training and inappropriate ways of enlisting team members often lead to unproductive planning.

---

### Signs of unhealthy team functioning:

- One or two team members doing all the talking and making the decisions
- Giving in to the false assumption that what a few members of the team feel or believe is what the entire team feels or believes
- An inability to disagree with other team members for fear of being "un-Christian"—a sign of a lack of trust and inability to confront the issues
- Team members who rarely show up at meetings—an indicator of a lack of commitment, or passion, for the ministry
- Team meetings in which members talk endlessly but seldom act—an inability to initiate, implement, and evaluate tasks
- A team that does not collaborate or communicate with other teams and organizations in the community of faith

---

Training for the CELT must occur on two levels. First, provide training for your team leaders, the chairperson and the co-chair. The CELT will not function effectively if the leader of the team is not aware of the leadership dynamics of effective teamwork. Second, the team members need to be trained on how to be good team members. We tend to think that members of church committees and teams naturally know how to be good members. This is not true. What they know is how to function as they have in the past. That's the problem! Many have sat through ineffective meetings that shaped their understanding of what it means to be a team member. The task at hand is to help your ministry area coordinators unlearn poor group or committee member behaviors so they can learn to work together effectively.

## Christian Education Leadership Team Members Ministry Descriptions

### *Ministry Description for the Christian Education Leadership Team Chairperson*

The chairperson of the CELT functions as coordinator and group facilitator. This person need not be "an educator" since the function of the chairperson is to run an effective meeting and help the team do its work. The chairperson sits on the chief coordinating leadership group in the church (e.g., the Church Council) and works closely with the pastoral or paid program staff.

Duties of the chairperson:

- Prepare and distribute the monthly agenda and communicate with the members of the CELT
- Support the members of the CELT in their work
- Lead the monthly CELT planning meetings
- Lead and oversee the initiation and progress of the assessment process
- Represent and interpret the work of the CELT on the Church Council
- Work with the Training Coordinator to plan, schedule, and provide for the training needs of the congregation
- Work with the ministry coordinators to recruit and recommend teachers, workers, and leaders for the congregation's Christian education formation programs
- Prepare a budget, with the staff resource person, for the Christian education formation ministry of the congregation
- Plan and conduct the annual CELT planning retreat

### *Ministry Description for the Christian Education Leadership Team Co-chair*

The co-chair of the CELT will assist the chairperson and will preside over the team when the chair is absent. The co-chair will assume the chairperson's seat when that person rotates off the CELT. The co-chair will serve as recorder for the group meetings and carry out assigned supportive administrative duties. The co-chair may serve on the Church Council or the coordinating body.

Duties of the co-chair:

- Record and distribute the minutes of the meetings and follow up with assignments
- Make room reservations and equipment arrangements for planned educational events
- Represent and interpret the work of the CELT on the Church Council and to the congregation when the chairperson is absent
- Maintain a record (e.g., a notebook) of the agendas and minutes of the CELT
- Assist the ministry area coordinators in their work of assessment and planning
- Assist the Sunday School Coordinator with recruiting and recommending teachers and workers for the Sunday School or church school program
- Assist in the planning and realization of the annual planning retreat
- Work with the childcare team or committee to arrange for childcare needs related to planned education events or programs

### Ministry Description for the Preschool Ministry Coordinator

The Preschool Ministry Coordinator will oversee and coordinate the preschool ministries and programs in the church. He or she works in conjunction with the CELT to plan, coordinate, and assess the preschool ministries and programs in the congregation.

Duties of the Preschool Ministry Coordinator:

- Work with the Sunday School Coordinator to recruit teachers and helpers for the preschool Sunday school department or church school
- Plan, with the members of the CELT, the preschool education ministry of the congregation
- Lead in the assessment of the preschool education formation ministry of the congregation
- Work with the Training Coordinator to provide for the training needs of teachers, workers, and leaders in the preschool ministry
- Work with the Training Coordinator to implement training to ensure compliance with the child protection policies as related to the preschool ministries

- Submit budget recommendations to the chairperson when requested
- Recruit volunteers and workers for the various preschool education ministry, programs, and events of the congregation
- Participate in the annual planning retreat

### Ministry Description for the Children's Ministry Coordinator

The Children's Ministry Coordinator oversees and coordinates the children's ministries and programs in the church. He or she works in conjunction with the CELT to plan, coordinate, and assess the children's ministries and programs in the congregation. In a smaller congregation, combine the positions of children and preschool ministries coordinators.

Duties of the Children's Ministry Coordinator:

- Work with the Sunday School Coordinator to recruit teachers and helpers for the children's church school or Sunday school department and classes
- Plan, with the members of the CELT, the children's education ministry of the congregation
- Lead in the assessment of the children's education formation ministry of the congregation
- Work with the Training Coordinator to provide for the training needs of teachers, workers, and leaders in the preschool ministry
- Work with the Training Coordinator to implement training to ensure compliance with the child protection policies as related to the children's ministries
- Submit budget recommendations to the chairperson when requested
- Recruit volunteers and workers for the various preschool education ministry, programs, and events of the congregation (summer camps, VBS, etc.)
- Recruit the Vacation Bible School Director in January, and begin to plan the VBS program
- Participate in the annual planning retreat

### Ministry Description for the Youth Ministry Coordinator

The Youth Ministry Coordinator oversees and coordinates the youth and student ministries and programs in the church. He or she works in conjunction with the church program staff person (the minister of youth or the youth pastor, for example) and with the CELT to plan, coordinate, and assess the youth ministry and its programs in the congregation.

Duties of the Youth Ministry Coordinator:

- Work with the Sunday School Coordinator to recruit teachers and helpers for the youth Sunday school department or church school classes
- Plan, with the members of the CELT, the youth education ministry of the congregation
- Lead in the assessment of the youth education formation ministry of the congregation
- Work with the Training Coordinator to provide for the training needs of teachers, workers, and leaders in the youth ministry
- Work with the Training Coordinator to implement training to ensure compliance with the child protection policies as related to the youth ministries
- Submit budget recommendations to the chairperson when requested
- Recruit volunteers and workers for the various youth education ministry, programs, and events of the congregation (retreats, mission trips, volunteering, special studies, etc.)
- Participate in the annual planning retreat

### Ministry Description for the Adult Ministry Coordinator

The Adult Ministry Coordinator oversees and coordinates the adult ministries and programs in the church. He or she works in conjunction with the church program staff person (the Minister of Education, the Pastor for Discipleship, or Minister of Spiritual Formation, for example) and with the CELT to plan, coordinate, and assess the adult ministries and programs in the congregation.

Duties of the Adult Ministry Coordinator:

- Work with the Sunday School Coordinator to recruit teachers and helpers for the adult Sunday school department, groups, and Bible study classes
- Plan, with the members of the CELT, the adult education ministry of the congregation
- Lead in the assessment of the adult education formation ministry of the congregation
- Work with the Training Coordinator to provide for the training needs of teachers, workers, and leaders in the adult ministry
- Submit budget recommendations to the chairperson when requested

- Recruit volunteers and workers for the various adult education ministry programs and events of the congregation (retreats, mission trips, volunteering, special studies, small groups, support groups, etc.)
- Participate in the annual planning retreat

### Ministry Description for the Sunday School Coordinator

The Sunday School Coordinator oversees and coordinates the Sunday school or church school program in the church. He or she works in conjunction with the church program staff person (the minister of education, the pastor for discipleship, or minister of spiritual formation, for example) and with the CELT to plan, coordinate, and assess the Sunday morning Bible study programs in the congregation.

Duties of the Sunday School Coordinator:

- Work with the members of the CELT to recruit teachers and volunteers for the Sunday school or church school.
- Plan, with the members of the CELT, the Sunday school and Bible studies education ministry of the congregation
- Oversee the orders for Sunday school resource literature, study materials, supplies, and equipment as needed
- Lead in the assessment of the Sunday school program as determined and scheduled by the Christian Education Leadership Team
- Work with the Training Coordinator to provide for the training needs of teachers, workers, and leaders in the Sunday school
- Submit budget recommendations to the chairperson when requested
- Recruit volunteers and workers for the various administrative needs of the Sunday school
- Plan and organize ministry programs and events of the Sunday school (rallies, special themes, picnics, retreats, Sunday school class mission projects, special studies, etc.)
- Participate in the annual planning retreat.

### Ministry Description for the Training Coordinator

The Training Coordinator works with the CELT to assess the training needs in the congregation and to provide the training events or programs as needed.

Duties of the Training Coordinator:

- Work with the members of the CELT
- Provide ongoing training for the CELT
- Work with the CELT to train teachers and volunteers for the Sunday school or church school
- Plan, with the members of the CELT, the training programs and events for the education ministry of the congregation
- Work with the CELT to implement training to ensure compliance with the child protection policies
- Lead in the assessment of the training needs of the Christian education formation program as determined by the CELT
- Submit budget recommendations to the chairperson when requested
- Recruit volunteers and workers for the various administrative needs of the training programs or events
- Participate in the annual planning retreat

## Conclusion

The philosophy behind the organizational structure of the CELT is that the congregation is a community of faith, and, therefore, its formal education programming must be integrated in its goals, themes, and corporate practices. The key to effective team leadership is enlisting the right people, training the team members, and facilitating integration. Training is critical to helping the team work effectively. Good teams don't just happen; they are cultivated. Effective teams are trained to understand the processes and practices of working together. Team members need to develop a culture of cooperation and mutual support. In the next chapter we'll explore in more detail the work of the CELT.

# 4

# The Work of the Christian Education Leadership Team

In this chapter we will explore in more detail the work of the Christian Education Leadership Team. Clarity about the work of the CELT, and its purpose and tasks, will help its members participate in the ministry of education more effectively. In subsequent chapters we will examine in more detail two of those responsibilities: planning and assessment.

## The Work of the Team

The function of the CELT is to plan, budget, coordinate, and evaluate the education ministry of the church. Although each person on the team has an area of specialization (preschool, children, youth, adults, or a particular program such as training or Sunday School), they work as a *team*. The team approach helps prevent people from working as Lone Rangers in their own areas of responsibility or programs. The team members work *together* in all phases of planning and leading the congregation's education programs and ministries.

Working together, the team coordinates the entire education enterprise, not just individual programs and events. The CELT works to oversee all the programs the church needs for educating in faith–retreats, special studies, training, and standard events, such as Vacation Bible School, etc. For example, it will work with the Sunday School Coordinator to ensure that the Sunday morning Bible study program meets the needs of the congregation's members and prospects. Since the Sunday School program is a major program in most churches, it merits having one person being responsible for overseeing it, but, again, not alone. Working together as a team not only facilitates a holistic and integrated education program, but it also adds synergy to the work, and support to the persons overseeing the various ministry areas. There is no better way to burn out passionate people than to make them believe, then require, that they are to work alone in carrying out a complex enterprise.

Mutual support becomes possible when the team works together with a common vision. For example, the Training Coordinator serves with the members of the CELT to identify and coordinate the training needs of the church when new programs are instituted, or when the team brings about a change in policy and procedure. Is childcare needed for an upcoming planned event? Are there enough trained childcare workers for the event? If not, the Training Coordinator is charged with providing training for childcare workers. Is the Vacation Bible School coming up in a few months? The training coordinator works with the CELT and/or the VBS Director to design, set up, and provide training for the VBS teachers and workers. Has the Sunday School Coordinator recruited new teachers? The Training Coordinator works with the team to schedule and provide new-teacher training. It is not necessary that the Training Coordinator conduct the training personally. He or she is merely responsible for seeing that the training events and programs are provided as needed.

### How to Be an Effective Team Leader

1. Manage time and meeting processes effectively
2. Provide team members with appropriate training
3. Provide resources for team members to aid them in their work
4. Check on the progress of assignments between meetings
5. Stay connected to team members
6. Thank team members for their work
7. Pray for team members

### Team Meetings

The CELT should meet monthly, with additional meetings as necessary, to plan and coordinate the congregation's education ministry. Planning and evaluation are ongoing processes. The chairperson and co-chair of the team will need to ensure that communication between team members and other leaders of the congregation is ongoing, for even after just a few missed meetings, the complex and multifaceted education ministry can begin to unravel.

The chairperson should develop an agenda to distribute to team members before each session. With this tool in hand, members of the team arrive at meetings better prepared to carry out the team's work. Appoint a recorder (usually the co-chair) to keep the minutes of the meeting. The recorder will prepare and distribute copies of the minutes to each team member. One copy will go into a permanent notebook or file. Conversations and decisions will be lost if minutes are not available in a permanent file. The minutes can help the team chairperson determine the agendas for future meetings.

### *How to Be an Effective Team Member*

1. Have a servant leader's spirit
2. Arrive at meetings on time
3. Share your opinions and listen to others
4. Do not dominate discussion
5. Do not become obsessed with a personal agenda
6. Carry out assignments thoroughly and within deadlines
7. Be prepared when asked to give a report

At the monthly meeting the CELT will coordinate and make final plans for the upcoming month's scheduled education events as well as evaluate the previous month's programming and events to ensure program effectiveness and see that things needing attention do not get ignored. Record in the minutes items that need to be addressed "the next time around," including recommendations for changes or improvement.

Typically, the chairperson will prepare the agenda in cooperation with the staff resource person. An agenda will help the team focus on its functions: planning, budgeting, coordinating, and evaluating, and will help it resist getting bogged down in attempts to "fix" a problem or to get distracted by issues on someone else's agenda. See the sample agenda on page 130 as a tool you might adopt for your team.

## The Annual Planning Retreat

Planning requires intentionality over a wide range of concerns—from day-to-day practices of the life of faith, to monthly meetings, to long-range planning. An annual planning retreat is helpful in laying the foundation for month-to-month planning. A focused time is necessary for developing new education ministries, redeveloping ministries that need renewal, assessing the current education ministry of the congregation, and casting vision for the church. Getting away to a location where team members can focus on long-range planning will energize the team in its work, build trust among members, and deepen relationships.

The key to an effective planning retreat is to focus on detailed planning a year-to-eighteen months in advance of implementation, and on general planning for long-range visioning (two-to-three years in advance). Planning a year in advance is a minimum time frame because it provides time to create a budget, secure resources and funding, enlist speakers for events, plan for missions and ministry service, promote congregational activities, and coordinate all aspects of congregational life. We will examine the planning process in more detail in chapter 6.

The CELT should meet for the planning retreat after the major church calendar is created. Working from the church calendar, the team will work toward creating an integrated education program that will focus on the emphases, cultural practices, and major events that will come up in the year. The basic calendar programming will be informed by the education and ministry goals of the church community. (If you do not have any education goals, then that is one place the team needs to start.) To be effective, team members must understand, and be supportive of, the identity and mission of the congregation and its vision for the future. They must know the congregation's history, understand its internal policies, and appreciate its culture. They also need to understand how the congregation's organizational structures and processes impact education programming. Those kinds of issues are difficult to deal with on a month-to-month basis in meetings, where attention to pragmatic programming and scheduling issues take priority, but are well-suited to an annual retreat.

An early task of a newly organized CELT will be to prepare and secure the congregation's approval of an education policy manual. (See appendix 2 for an outline of an education policy manual.) This lengthy and challenging project will prove to be one of the most helpful resources for the team as it continues to develop. Nothing bogs down a task group as much as having to reinvent the wheel every year or solve the same problems again and again. One of the first major policies should be an updating or creating of a child protection policy for the preschool, children's, and youth ministries.

If the issues related to education policies, procedures, procurement, and budgeting in congregational life are unclear, the CELT would be wise to discuss, define, and reach agreement with the clergy staff and lay leaders on the following issues:

- Shared theology of church and the nature of *the Church* as congregation. Is the church more like a school or a community of faith? The answer to this question will determine the kind of planning needed.
- The educational philosophy that best fits the culture of the congregation and the goals of the education programs.[1]
- Leadership teams, committees, or groups that will assist the CELT in carrying out its mission. The goal is to determine ways of integrating the ministry of Christian education and to assess whether the congregation's organizational structures and practices are congruent with its mission.
- The scope and responsibility of the CELT for the planning and coordination of the church's education programs related to their functions of setting education policies, administrative procedures, procurement, and budgeting. The effectiveness of the CELT is directly proportional to the degree to which these issues are clearly understood. One of the frustrations of congregational life occurs when a team is held responsible for tasks without clear guidelines from which to work. Teams must understand what they are being asked to do, what theology informs their functioning, the authority they have to make decisions, and what policies or boundaries guide and/or limit their work.

---

### How to Lead an Effective Meeting

1. Begin the meeting on time
2. Distribute the agenda to team members prior to the meeting
3. Give team members the opportunity to add items to the agenda
4. Record the minutes of each meeting

5. Distribute minutes to team members after each meeting
6. Keep team members on task
7. Encourage all team members to share their opinions
8. Do not allow any team member to dominate discussion
9. Make assignments with timely deadlines
10. End the meeting on time

## Budgeting

One important function of the CELT is developing a budget, recommending it to the church body, and evaluating policies and procedures for procurement and budgeting related to the church's education ministries. The responsibility for making budget decisions belongs to all of the team members, but the task of crafting the budget can be assigned to one or two members—for example, the chairperson and the staff resource person, or the co-chair and the staff resource person. It is logical to include the staff resource person as a part of this process since he or she will serve as a liaison to other groups involved in the budgeting process. This will help ensure that fiscal processes and timetables are considered.

The budget should be both adequate for the current ministry and able to facilitate program development. Most congregations do not fund their education programs to even "maintenance" level (somewhere around 2–3 percent of the total church ministry budget—excluding salaries for staff, workers, sitters, etc.). Planning on a three-year cycle helps formulate a budget that is geared toward development. If your team decides this year you need within two years to create a new education program component for your ministry to families, then you know to increase your budget to allow for new curricular resources, training new volunteers, increasing childcare staffing, and program development related to space, equipment, supplies, and other resources.

## Coordinating

The results of a lack of ministry coordination in congregational life can be compared to a biological process. Without oversight and regulation of the whole body, isolated small groups often emerge that negatively impact the entire congregational system. Like disconnected cells, they seek their own goals and often lose sight of corporate needs. Compartmentalization becomes a way of life. Church leaders focus on the trees rather than the forest. Collaboration, integration, and mutual support toward a common good are sacrificed.

One important function of the CELT is to cultivate the collaborative and integrated nature of education for the faith community. Sometimes a congregation needs a specific focus for the body as a whole. The CELT can help determine when such a focus is needed. For example, if the team determines that the members of the congregation are underdeveloped in their prayer life, it can plan a prayer emphasis that will involve members of all ages in the church. If Christian stewardship is an issue of urgency in a particular year, the team will give attention to that emphasis in programming. If response to a local issue or social crisis forces the congregation to focus on a particular theological question about its stance and response, the team can give attention to finding ways for the congregation to address that need through its education programming. The life of the church is its curriculum, and the CELT's responsibility is to develop that curriculum and coordinate the ways in which that curriculum can happen.

A CELT needs to ensure that the congregation's spiritual "diet" is balanced. Focusing on subject content–ethics, history, doctrine, Bible study, prayer, worship, etc., is one approach for assessing the congregation's education diet. Focusing on the developmental needs of the members is another–addressing what children, youth, and adults need at particular critical stages of the life cycle. A third way is to focus on the educational needs of the congregation's varied programs–not just the Sunday school, but also missions organizations, discipleship, music and worship ministries, and ministry and service committees or teams. Since "everything we do is Christian education," no area of congregational life is not Christian formation.

In chapter 6 we will recommend the Christian Church Year as the rubric for education planning that will facilitate a community of faith approach to Christian education. This rubric promotes a framework for learning for the whole body that makes educational integration of programs, events, and themes more natural. When the entire congregation is focused on the binding "Story" of the community, it is easier for persons of all ages to create meaning through their shared experiences. Life together through the Christian story becomes the "curriculum" that brings balance in the life of the congregation.

An informing theology (our understanding of God), ecclesiology (our understanding of the Church), and pedagogy (our understanding of how people learn) should inform how the CELT goes about its planning process. The extent to which these three areas are intentionally integrated is the extent to which planning becomes effective. Asking, "What are the theology, ecclesiology, and pedagogy that inform this planning?" will keep the CELT on track. The team should also ask, "What are the values that inform the planning needs of the congregation?"

Planning must involve theological reflection for all aspects of congregational life–the true curriculum: life together and the corporate practices of the members in community. The CELT will be prepared to address the corporate spiritual needs of congregational life when it has a clear understanding of theology, ecclesiology, and pedagogy, and gives attention to the influence of all aspects of congregational life of its members.

## Conclusion

Ultimately, the effectiveness of the CELT is measured by how well persons in the community of faith are growing in their faith and are living out their calling in obedience to God through worshiping God and ministering to others. The CELT must work toward engaging members in the practice of discipleship and in the practice of ministry. The question, "How are members of our congregation growing in their ministry service?" is a helpful assessment. In chapter 7 we will address the evaluative and assessment function of the Christian Education Leadership Team. In that chapter you will find a plan for assessing your Christian education formation program.

# 5

# Education Formation Approaches in Congregations

This chapter will serve as a guide to help the CELT provide a more balanced offering of education opportunities for the members of the congregation. As your CELT plans the congregation's education ministry, it will need to address more than the issue of *what* to do by way of programs, events, and experiences, and *when* to offer them. It must also determine *how* it will carry out Christian education formation. In this chapter we will identify, define, and describe various educational approaches for Christian education formation. Learning to identify specific approaches and their dynamics will enable you to choose and use those approaches most capable of helping your congregation move closer to a faith community formation approach to Christian education.

You will learn to match content areas with appropriate corresponding approaches and methodologies for learning. The challenges for congregational educators are to: (1) identify the appropriate education goals (concepts and beliefs, behaviors and practices, values) desired in the lives of congregational members, (2) accurately identify the education approach congruent to those outcomes, (3) plan and implement the educational means that will actually bring about the desired Christian education formation outcomes, and (4) assess the effectiveness of the congregation's programs and activities. This chapter will help address these issues so your education planning is both intentional and effective.

## Different Ways of Learning

People are fond of saying things such as, "You can't learn to ride a bike by reading a book," or, "The only way to learn to swim is by jumping in the pool." Such axioms are evidence we intuitively understand that a person can learn in different ways and that different things must be learned in certain ways. Christian education formation through the community of faith approach calls for appreciation and implementation of different ways of learning. Certain kinds of learning are accessible only by engaging in particular kinds of communal practices. Problems arise when a community of faith tries to fit Christian education into exclusively instructional models and thus to limit it to cognitive content or to a classroom setting. In English the term "to know" does not sufficiently distinguish between different kinds of knowledge. Other languages employ multiple words to describe differentiated ways of knowing: French (*savoir* vs. *connaitre*), Spanish (*conocer* vs. *saber*), German (*kennen* vs. *wissen*), and Latin (*cognoscere* vs. *scire*). In each case the second term refers to knowledge by description, which is used to explain and share *about* an experience. The first term, by contrast, is knowledge by acquaintance. Knowledge by acquaintance is acquired *directly* and involves the emotions. We refer to it as relational knowledge. This type of knowledge highlights the difference between knowing *about* someone because of what we have been told and *knowing* someone because we have a relationship with that person. Too many experiences of Christian education focus on propositional knowledge as if Christianity were nothing else. One can know all *about* Christ and still not know him relationally. Certainly, comprehension of the core narrative of the faith is essential to the Christian life, but reason will only get one so far on the journey of faith. When a congregation practices didactic instructional approaches almost exclusively, they stand in danger of convincing their church members that Christianity is more about *what you know* than it is about *whom you know.*

The move from traditional schooling approaches to communal-corporate approaches will shift the focus of learning at many levels. Specifically, a community-of-faith approach will cause a move:

- from teacher-focused methods to learner-centered methods,
- from teacher-dependent to learner-motivated learning,
- from content transmission (instruction) to discovery learning (discernment and self-understanding),

- from passive listening in a classroom to active participation in the life of community,
- from externally focused learning of concepts to internally focused learning for self-understanding,
- from content-focused instruction to relationship-mediated experiences,
- from strictly individual practices of faith to greater participation in corporate formative practices of faith,
- from teaching for knowledge attainment to learning for obedience for the practice of ministry and missions in and through the community of faith.

By planning for the ways of knowing and learning most authentic for acquiring faith and by applying the right *approaches to learning faith,* we can facilitate meaningful learning for our members. We need consistently to make available to our members those learning approaches most congruent with *the ways people actually acquire faith.*

Advocating a move away from schooling approaches toward more communal-corporate ways of learning is not to suggest that we should abandon educational approaches associated primarily with schooling. Even basic instruction for knowledge acquisition has its place in the congregation. What we strive for in our planning is a more balanced repertoire in the use of the ways of learning. Remember, however, that the job of the CELT is to plan and coordinate the overall program (curriculum) of the congregation, not to micromanage lesson plans or over-monitor the content of the programs. Those are left up to the persons entrusted with, and trained in, leading the programs or teaching the classes. The CELT focuses on the big picture, and, therefore, limits its scope to the fundamental concerns such as educational philosophy, approaches, structures, format, and process. Figure 5-1 defines each of those categories, illustrates how each is derivative of the others, and adds procedure, method, and technique.

### Figure 5-1: Categories of Education Practice

| CATEGORY | DEFINITION | EXAMPLES |
|---|---|---|
| Philosophy | A particular system of thought that holds a systematic position of basic concepts such as truth, existence, reality, causality, and freedom. | Constructivism Pragmatism Perennialism |

| Approach | An informed and particular way of going about the educational enterprise congruent with one's philosophical stance. | Religious Instruction<br>Interpretation<br>Dialogical Learning<br>Praxis-Reflection<br>Training<br>Sponsorship<br>Apprenticeship<br>Mentoring<br>Direction and Spiritual Friendships<br>Intergenerational<br>Communal (nurture, fellowship, rites & rituals, practices)<br>Matching approaches with content and programs (see Figure 5-3) |
|---|---|---|
| Structure | The arrangement of and relations between the parts or elements of the educational approach. | The planning structure used by the CELT is "centralized." |
| Format | A particular arrangement of the educational enterprise at whatever level. In the example, the level of a lesson. | • Beginning: Teacher lectures<br>• Middle: Students research (discovery learning)<br>• End: Student presentations and teacher assessments |
| Process | A series of interrelated actions or steps taken to achieve a particular end. Processes tend to be open-ended and cyclical. | Planning, Preparation, Execution, Review, Evaluation, Planning, etc. |
| Procedure | An established or official way of doing something, a series of actions conducted in a certain order or manner. Procedures tend to be linear. | Procedure for Sunday School faculty development:<br>1. Advertise<br>2. Recruit & call<br>3. Train & mentor<br>4. Practice<br>5. Evaluate<br>6. Assign to a class |
| Method | A particular form of procedure for accomplishing the desired learning objectives. | Small group<br>Lecture<br>Reading source materials<br>Listening to recording<br>Testing |
| Technique | A particular way of executing a method, or a subset of a method in the actual act of teaching-learning. | Question and answer<br>Behavior desist<br>Presenting an objective<br>Providing lesson closure |

Focus the work of your CELT on the more foundational areas. Resist trying to micromanage issues of teaching methods, classroom techniques, or teaching proceedures. The function of the team is planning, coordinating, and assessing the overall education program of the congregation according to your church's vision, ensuring a focus on integration, communal practices, and on the Christian Church Year.

### Moving Toward a Community-of-Faith Approach to Christian Education Formation

Attempting to change the way we do Christian education in our congregations is difficult, but we must move toward more appropriate ways of teaching if we want the experience of learning in church to move toward formation education. Let us examine how to move toward an approach that taps into faith formation approaches to Christian education. Using Figure 5-2: "A Community of Faith Approach to Christian Education Formation," we will examine how shifting to certain methods and approaches work better for learning as formation. Refer to the diagram on page 63 as you review the explanation below.

The large circle represents the context in which education for Christian formation takes place: the congregation as a community of faith. Communities are "bounded," meaning they have a sense of who "belongs" and who does not. Congregations determine who "belongs" by various means: by familial relationship in family-sized patriarchal-matriarchal congregations or by official membership rosters, but, also, sometimes by level of participation. Learners within the congregation have significant formation relationships on several levels: congregational-communal, small groups, families, and individual. The top dashed line that runs through the boundary of the circle demonstrates that the congregation exists in the context of the world and of a community, and, as such, often shares and reflects the values and culture of its context. The dotted line (second from the top) that cuts across the boundary circle highlights the movement across the spectrum of educational approaches we can use in teaching all populations and groups within the congregation. The poles are from "Schooling" on the left to "Learning through Obedience" at the right end of the spectrum. All approaches have their use in educating people in the context of a congregation, but, as we will see, some are more essential to faith formation than others.

### Figure 5-2: A Community of Faith Approach to Christian Education Formation

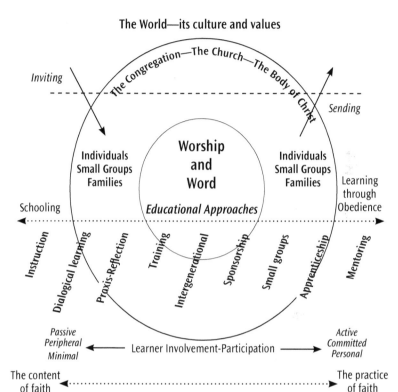

Two basic congregational movements are illustrated on the chart: "inviting" those outside of the church into its fellowship and "sending" those within the church to engage the world. The corresponding educational movements are traditionally termed "the journey inward" and "the journey outward." A holistic approach to Christian education will facilitate movement in both directions, helping members move inward toward full involvement in the center of community life *and* sending members out into the world to engage in ministry and missions in the name of Christ.

At the center of the diagram appears "Worship & Word." Theologically, these are at the core of a church community's theology and identity. In this example, these elements represent the core values that inform the church's mission and vision. Subsequently, these shape its understanding of Christian education for the formation of its community members and participants. A church can substitute other components to reside at the informing center of the congregation, depending on its theology and identity. For example, a church can choose to place at the center: worship and fellowship; praise and mission; God and mission; Jesus and service; or proclamation and outreach. In most churches Christian education enterprises are not only "broken" in methodology (using the wrong means for the intended ends), but also in a lack of clarity of their theology, philosophy of education, and corporate communal identity. The work of an authentic and viable Christian education formation program begins here.

If your CELT does not know the theology and education philosophy that informs your church's programs, then how can you decide which methods are most appropriate, which educational approaches are most suited to your community, or what programs you will offer? How will you be able to discern when a teaching method is not congruent with the goals and values of Christian teaching?

The two double-arrowheaded lines at the bottom of the diagram illustrate how movement away from approaches of Schooling and instruction toward education formation (and ultimately toward learning through obedience) affects how students respond to learning. The first solid line labeled "Learner Involvement-Participation" shows that methods plotted on the left end of the spectrum yield a learner posture that is passive, requires minimal participation, and offers content that is of peripheral concern to the learner. As educational approaches and methods are used that correspond with a movement toward the right side of the spectrum, the learner is required to be more active, more committed, and to value personally both the content and process of learning. The powerful truth here is that the education enterprise is formative—consistent exposure to one type of educational approach will produce a particular kind of learner. So, a steady diet of methods representative of those on the left side of the diagram will produce, in the end, passive learners, with minimal commitment to the content and experience of learning in matters of faith.

The dashed double-arrowheaded line below the solid "Learner Involvement-Participation" line illustrates that methods on the left end of the spectrum (for example, "Instruction") are more concerned with the "content of faith," while those methods plotted toward the right side of the spectrum (for example, "Mentoring") are concerned with the "practice of faith." In fact, methods on the right side of the spectrum *are* the practices of faith!

Along the "Educational Approaches" line are nine examples of learning approaches across the spectrum from Schooling to Learning through Obedience. (We could plot other approaches but we will use these nine as examples.) Any number of teaching methods and programs can be used under each approach–some being more appropriate to the goals and objectives of the learning enterprise for each. For example, for education goals related to content mastery of concepts, knowledge, and Bible content, the methods related to Instruction are the appropriate ones to use. Under that approach we can plot classroom experiences, Sunday school, Bible studies, and book or topical studies. Let us examine these approaches in some detail.

## A Survey of Congregational Approaches to Education

The following approaches offer a wide-ranging repertoire for planning the Christian education formation program for your congregation. Each serves its purpose in bringing about a certain type of learning. Some are suitable for many contexts, while others are effective only in a few. For example, religious instruction can be the dedicated educational approach of a particular program, such as a Bible school, or can be one component used in a program that uses other complimentary approaches, as in an intergenerational Vacation Bible School. Some approaches are narrow to the extent that they are applicable only in a certain context or for a particular set of learning outcomes.

Here is a review of a selected number of educational approaches. We will define and describe them first. Then we will identify the type of content and context for which each is most suitable.

### Religious Instruction

Religious instruction is a way of teaching based on the social science disciplines of teaching and learning, such as education and developmental psychology, and theories of learning. The practice of religious instruction can involve basic transmissive goals (acquiring knowledge, learning *about* something) to very sophisticated ends. A key characteristic is that it is highly teacher-dependent and content-focused.

James Michael Lee was a chief proponent for a more transformative end to religious instruction–namely, holistic Christian living as the major goal of Christian religious education.[1] In many churches, instruction constitutes the exclusive form of education offered in formal programs. In addition, lack of teacher training causes much of that instruction to be done poorly and ineffectively.

## Dialogical Learning

A number of interpersonal learning processes are possible only in small groups. These learning processes can foster the kind of learning that brings about change in the life of the learner.

Dialogical learning is a structured, intentional process that leads to insights and deep understanding and, ultimately, application in the life of the learner.[2] The process of dialogical learning in the small group can work with whatever subject or content your programs may want to offer: a Bible passage, a theological or life topic, a book, an article, a concept, etc.

*Dialogue* is not synonymous with *discussion*. People tend to use the words *dialogue* and *discussion* interchangeably, so that making a distinction between the two often yields resistance.

In a discussion you try to put forth, or achieve, a definitive point of view, while in dialogue one strives for insight. Dialogue requires listening to another person's point of view with appreciation and seeking understanding through empathy and reflection. Discussion seeks to persuade and convince others. Its goal is for all the members to come to agreement on one meaning. It is used to evaluate and select the best or the most acceptable perspective in the group, or to affirm, justify, and defend one's assumptions. The distinction between dialogue and discussion is not subtle.

## Praxis-Reflection

The act of reflection on one's experience to make meaning is one of the most critical practices of the Christian life. Sharing with others on a deeper level, reflecting on our experiences of life and faith (and bringing a faith-spiritual-theological frame of reference to them) is one of the most transformative ways of educating in faith. The praxis-reflection approach involves both reflection and action. "The process of transformation as praxis implicit in this model suggests a dialectic movement in which reflection and action constantly interact to produce a different consciousness and a different action upon the world."[3]

The praxis-reflection approach can be used as the key component in a number of Christian education formation programs, including mission projects or experiences. Congregations do well in offering mission trip opportunities for their members. Experiences in and of themselves have no inherent meaning. Theological reflection on one's experience addresses the question of God's action through us, and participation with us. Such reflection results in meaning and a change in consciousness–the ways we think about ourselves and the world. An ideal application of the praxis-reflection approach is to offer reflection on a biblical text, theological concept, or corporate value of the faith community in preparation for the mission project. That is followed by the experience of participating in the practice of mission framed by the text, theological concept, or value. The mission project is followed with an opportunity to reflect on the experience to interpret and articulate its meaning, both personal (what this experience means to me) and corporate (what it means that I participated in this experience as a member of my community of faith). Ultimately, the question is not so much how we changed the world through the experience, but how God changed us.

## Training

Training deals primarily with building skills rather than acquiring content knowledge. Skills acquisition through training can span the simple to the complex and usually involves striving for achieving competence or mastery. Think of all of the many practices or actions in the congregation that fall under the category of "how to...," and you have identified a potential area for training. Training can involve everything from how to teach a class, how to usher, how to count the offering receipts, how to use your Bible, how to change a baby's diaper in the nursery, how to make the coffee for Sunday School, how to sing in the choir, to how to handle the sound systems, and everything in between.

For the training process to be effective, its education principles must be followed rigorously, as is true with every educational approach. Effective training programs follow basic components:

- They have clear objectives;
- They assess the learner's skill level and ability at the beginning of the training process;
- They use appropriate methodology (e.g., skills attainment vs. information attainment);
- They model the skill at the level for skill mastery;
- They provide opportunity for practice and feedback;

- They provide opportunity for competence and improvement;
- They assess the learner's progress during and at the end of training in light of objectives.

Training is an ongoing process. For learners to move from competence to mastery, they must rehearse skills. As congregational programs and tasks become more complex or evolve, persons must be retrained to effectively manage the new dimensions of the job or ministry.

## Sponsorship

Like many teaching relationships, sponsorship can range from formal to informal, but, typically, sponsorship is a relationship connected in some way to a larger community or organization. Sponsorship is one person helping another in navigating some facet of community life–such as an entry point for membership–as guide, advisor, and supporter. A sponsor assumes responsibility for another person, or a group, during a period of instruction, apprenticeship, or probation. Sponsorship implies endorsement and thus some expectation for reciprocal accountability. Since a sponsor must vouch for the suitability of a candidate, the relationship involves a high level of trust and hope. In faith communities sponsorship often involves an established member and a candidate for baptism, confirmation, or membership in the church or in a facet of church life, such as a ministry or a program. Sponsorship is not just a teaching relationship between two individuals. This relationship involves the entire community and requires clarity about the community's values and beliefs and about what the community values in its members. In some churches the role of a godparent is an example of sponsorship.

## Apprenticeship

Apprenticeship in the congregational setting involves helping a person move from a novice level to mastery in communal skills, functions, or practices. Education in the congregational context is always social. The goal of Christian education formation is to help the congregation "be a spiritual community that forms people of faith."[4] Apprenticeship is often confused with "mentoring," but they are not the same. Apprenticeship is a form of training (today mostly associated with internships). Its focus is on "the way to do things" in a specific context. When you invite a person to work alongside another in a church ministry to "learn the ropes" or when you seek out a person to teach you the way things are done in your particular setting, that's apprenticeship. Effective apprenticeship also teaches "why we do things this way" and in that way inculcates communal values and memory into the learner as a member of the community. Learning under apprenticeship is not just a matter of learning how to do it, but also, "This is how *we* do it."

## Mentoring

Mentoring seems to have a romantic hold on people's imagination. It is easily confused with training, apprenticeships, coaching, internships, modeling, "spiritual friendships," or other "learning relationships."

We define mentoring as: a vocational relationship that takes place in the context of the situated practice of a vocation. Mentoring is about introducing someone into a vocation.

Mentoring has these characteristics:

- A bounded relationship (the mentor-mentee roles) that has a narrow window for when it begins and when it ends.
- A *volitional* relationship—persons must choose to enter into it. Making mentoring an "assignment" or a requirement in a program ignores this important dynamic.
- An introduction into the guild of a profession, the proctored mastery of vocational skills required in that profession.
- A developmental component—namely, it is for those at the entry point of vocation, not for those *in preparation* for a vocation. Those being mentored need to be young adults (emphasis on *adults*), not adolescents or post-adolescents or those in a state of protracted adolescence.

Much of what people do under the rubric of "mentoring" is not appropriate to their goals or context, is not applicable to their audience, and is not designed to be mentoring at all. It is not appropriate to define something such as parenting as a "vocation" and then create a program that provides elder "mentors" to young parents. You certainly cannot "mentor" children or youth. Maintaining a rigorous understanding of the nature of the mentoring relationship can challenge uncritical notions about "mentoring" that render its attempt ineffective.

## Small Groups, Support Groups, Group Spiritual Direction

A further move from individual-centered to more corporate ways of learning is the small groups approach. This approach covers a broad range of formats and learning modalities, from study groups or support groups to group spiritual direction. Small groups can be long or short term, and open or closed. While small groups programming becomes a necessity in larger congregations, it remains a vital way of educating in faith even in smaller congregations. Small groups facilitate more intimate interpersonal relationships, encourage active participation by each member, require a higher level of accountability of those in the group, and help shift the learning dynamic from teacher-centered to learner-focused. The experience of being together in formative relationships becomes the modality for learning.

Pragmatic guidelines for planning will help you determine when to start new small groups:

- Plan to have seven small groups for every 100 active members in the congregation (Sunday School class, Bible study group, support group, spiritual direction group, etc.).
- Plan for ways of getting every new member into a small group within three to six months of his or her joining the church. (Assign someone on the CELT to track this.)
- In a congregation with 150 to 300 active members, 20 percent of small groups should have been started within the past two years.

### Intergenerational Education

Intergenerational education is primarily an approach, not a program. Some programs can facilitate it, like VBS, retreats, churchwide festivals, corporate worship, mission or service projects, etc. The primary pedagogical dynamic of the intergenerational approach is: *everybody learns the same thing at the same time together.* Attention to the intergenerational approach to congregational practices can facilitate the concept of church life as curriculum. We need to be intentional about tapping into the intergenerational component of our congregation's communal practices: worship, rites, and rituals. This is often difficult in our individualistic culture. For example, baptisms, weddings, the Lord's supper, funerals, and corporate worship are all primarily communal intergenerational events. Often they are conducted and perceived as if the individual is at the center of the practice. It behooves the pastoral leader officiating at these communal events to begin by saying, "Before we begin, I just want to remind you that this is not about you."

Framing our Christian education formation planning from a community-of-faith approach means that we pay greater attention to the intergenerational nature of being church together. Communities are, by nature, inter- and intra-generational. This is part of a community's important function of being generative–of passing its values, beliefs, and identity to the next generation. Every corporate practice, every communal gathering must be approached from an intergenerational viewpoint: everyone in the community, of whatever age and generation, is participating together. Being attentive to the generative nature of corporate gatherings will mean that we give more attention to the use of narrative, including stories. Communal gatherings are optimum times for telling "Our Story" (the grand biblical story of God's people of faith), of telling our congregation's story as a local community of faith, and inviting people to tell the stories of their lives. In this way we not only instill and perpetuate communal memory, but we also identify those points of intersection among the three narratives of the faith of our members (the biblical "Story," the story of our congregation as community, and the individual life story of each member)–individually and corporately.

We examined a congregational history timeline that a church had created as a way to illustrate and recall for its members the church's corporate story. On it were marked nodal events such as the calling of its pastors, the dates when buildings were erected, and other significant events in the life of the congregation. Members had been invited to mark on the timeline events they remembered as significant. Some entered the dates of the deaths of founding members. Others added in episodes of crises and celebrations. At one point along the timeline, in a child's handwriting, was scrawled, "Doug comes to FBC." We were very struck by that entry. It was a dramatic example of the meaningful intersection of the multigenerational story of the congregation with the life of this young child. In effect, he was declaring, "This is where I entered the story. I'm a part of this church's story–and its story is a part of me."

## Learning through Obedience

An informing theology that guides the life of the Christian congregation is that our faith and practice are not just about us. Isaiah makes clear that God is not interested in our worship if it is just about us and not about others (Isa. 1:10–20). A product of worship is to launch us into God's redemptive work–ministry to others. The Church cannot fulfill its ultimate purpose of pleasing God through worship without also living a life of love. God is pleased when our act of worship causes us to live a life of obedience that is expressive of God's nature of love. Proper worship of God transforms us so that God can work through us for the sake of others. In a real sense we become the presence of God to others. Being the people of God means being who God has created us to be and doing what God has called us to do. Worship and ministry are, therefore, integrated. They cannot be separated.

Opportunities for participation in ministry and missions are the most effective faith-shaping activities that congregations can offer. Research from the Search Institute discovered that youth are best shaped when they are engaged in ministry to others—especially when they experience that ministry with their families.[5] I vividly recall one of the most meaningful experiences of my early teenage years. During a local missions experience our church built a modest house for an eighty-five-year-old woman on Lady's Island, South Carolina. I will never forget the house in which she lived before we built the house—an old, dirt-floored, one-room shack leaning to the side. Light from the outside streamed in through the cracks in the plank boards. Inside sat the woman on the only chair in the house. On one side of the room were several blankets stacked neatly on the dirt floor where she slept each night. There was one metal cooking pot resting on bricks in the fireplace, but no electricity, no running water, and no bathroom.

Every evening for several weeks I jumped into the truck with my dad and brother to travel to the mission site. Each day I anticipated the excitement of participating in this project of love along with other church members. In the course of time we built this woman a new house with a bathroom, electricity, and running water. It was the first time in my life that I recall having a meaningful purpose beyond my own immediate needs. I had been nurtured by the church and my family from my birth. Church was a way of life for us. From my early years of life I had learned about God, the Bible, and the stories of faith. I had that knowledge in my mind, but it was not until that mission experience that the knowledge in my mind found its way to my heart. I experienced what it meant to love others in practice, not just as an abstract idea, and deep down in the depths of my soul I felt the affirming presence of God at work in me. To this day I believe that what Christians most need does not come from a classroom experience. It comes as a result of believers working together in living out God's calling to participate in the redemptive works of Christ in the world through the church.

## Matching Approaches with Content and Programs

When planning the Christian education formation programs in the congregation, strive to match the education approaches with their corresponding content. (See Figure 5-3, which illustrates this matching.) Additionally, give attention to the roles of the student and teacher based on the approach you select as you plan programs and events.

Use the "Balance of Repertoire" worksheet at the end of this chapter to assess how well your education programs apply a balanced repertoire of education approaches.

### Moving toward Communal-Congregational Planning

All of the educational approaches mentioned in this chapter have their appropriate use in the congregational context. Your CELT should feel free to make the best use of each approach as appropriate to the education goals you desire. Keep in mind, however, that some things in the Christian faith are never learned through instruction–they are learned only in community, through relationships, and by obedience. In much of the Christian life, faith is acquired by obeying *first;* only then will insight follow obedience.

Let us recall two scenarios from the gospels. In the first, a crowd surrounds Jesus. Some are followers, some are disciples, and some are the curious who have come to hear Jesus preach and teach. Jesus, the master teacher, teaches the crowd by telling about the birds of the air and the lilies of the field–how they do not toil or work, but yet, how God cares for them. He tells the people that their loving Father in heaven cares for them even more than these, and tells them, therefore, "Do not worry, saying, 'What shall we eat?' or 'What shall we drink?' or 'What shall we wear?'" (Mt. 6:31). The crowd is inspired. Doubtless, many are moved, and others walk away saying, "What a wonderful speaker!"

Now recall a second scene. Jesus gathers his intimate small group of disciples. He sends them on a mission with these instructions: "Take nothing for the journey except a staff–no bread, no bag, no money in your belts. Wear sandals but not an extra tunic." (Mk. 6:8–9). The disciples obey and return reporting the great works they were able to do in God's name.

The important pedagogical question is: Who do you think really learned to trust God? Was it the people in the large crowds who heard a great sermon and were "inspired"? Or was it the *small group* of disciples who, because of their *relationship* with Jesus, and because they *obeyed first,* even without fully understanding, *experienced* God's provision?

**Figure 5-3: Corresponding Components for Educational Approaches**

| | DESCRIPTION | ROLE OF THE TEACHER | ROLE OF THE LEARNER | APPROPRIATE CONTENT | SAMPLE PROGRAMS |
|---|---|---|---|---|---|
| Religious Instruction | Understanding "about" things; comprehension about concepts under study | Instructor Lecturer Classroom manager Learning engineer | Novice Concept mastery | Concepts, principles, knowledge | Sunday School Bible study Topical course |
| Dialogical Learning | Structured intentional process for understanding, insight, and application | Prompter Facilitator Guide for the group learning experience | Active participant in learning through dialogue | Concepts, principles, self-knowledge, experiences | Bible or book study |
| Praxis-Reflection | Learning through guided experiences and through reflection and action | Experience planner Coach Guide Supervisor Prompter | Active participant in experiences, reflection, and action | Self-knowledge, experiences, interpretation, action | Missions experiences Ministry experiences |
| Training | Acquiring skills and moving toward increased mastery | Expert Trainer Model Evaluator | Novice acquiring expertise and mastery in particular skill | Skills and knowledge specific to practice | Ushering Teaching Tech support Ministries |
| Sponsorship | Reciprocal relationship of encouragement and introduction or induction into community | Endorser Godparent Guide Sponsor | One introduced into membership or aspect of communal life | Self-understanding, the community's practices, values, and norms | Baptisms Programs Groups |

| Approach | Description | Teacher Role | Learner Role | Content | Setting |
|---|---|---|---|---|---|
| Apprenticeship | Learning in relationship from and alongside an expert | Model<br>Expert<br>Guide<br>Evaluator | Novice acquiring expertise and mastery in a practice or guild | Skills, knowledge specific to practice and discipline or job | Ministry or missions group<br>Guilds |
| Mentoring | A bounded learning vocational relationship | Mentor<br>Guide<br>Expert<br>Teacher | Novice introduced into a vocation | Self-understanding, the vocation and its context | Any vocational setting |
| Small Groups | Learning in the context of a group of persons (4-18 persons) with common interests and high accountability to a mutual interest | Teacher<br>Process manager<br>Resource<br>Prompter<br>Facilitator | Member and participant in the group learning process | Whatever is at the center of the focus and purpose of the group | Bible study<br>Support group<br>Book study<br>Fellowship |
| Intergenerational | Learning in a communal context in which everyone learns the same thing at the same time together | Experience engineer<br>Prompter<br>Guide<br>Interpreter<br>Generative | Participant and learner in relationship with others | Knowledge and appreciation of the community, its practices, beliefs, values, and norms | Primarily in any corporate gathering of communal practices<br>VBS and other intergenerational programs |
| Learning through obedience | The stance and practice of putting faith in action, which assumes that insight and learning follow the act of obedience; "obey to learn" rather than "learn to obey" | Spiritual guide<br>Encourager<br>Model<br>Companion | Disciple and participant in the practices of faith and in the practice of ministry | The "practices of faith" is the content of learning; self-insight and self-knowledge as a disciple of Christ | Ministries<br>Spiritual direction<br>Mission trips and events<br>Spiritual disciplines |

## Conclusion

Some things in the Christian life are learned only through experiences and relationships, because relationships mediate growth in the life of faith. For the kind of relationships that help persons grow in faith in the learning context, corporate and communal learning is necessary. One of the biggest failures of current Christian education is the assumption that one can plant insight into passive learners that will result in "transference of learning." We have known for years that much of what is learned in "church school" makes little difference in the lives of learners. Why, then, do we continue to insist on schooling people in faith?

Where do we find a more authentic and meaningful way to teach those things that are at the heart of the Christian faith? We find the answer in using the life of the congregation as a primary approach to planning for Christian education formation. Using the church life as our curriculum will help shift our ways of helping people learn from a passive posture to active engagement; from a peripheral concern with Bible truths to active application through experience and practices; from dependence on others to taking responsibility for one's values and convictions; from peripheral membership to fuller participation in the life of the church community.

If we want to make Christian education a transforming influence in the lives of our members, then we need to use methods that move away from exclusively instructional approaches that focus on *teaching,* and move toward approaches that emphasize *learning in community through relationships and religious practices.* We must take seriously the conviction that in order to be authentic Christian educators, the methodology of Christian education we use needs to be authentically Christian.

## Balance of Repertoire Wooksheet

An effective congregational Christian education program uses a broad repertoire of educational approaches appropriate to the program goals. Assess how well your congregation uses a broad repertoire by ranking how often you use the approaches with the identified age groups: 1=Never 2=Rarely 3=Sometimes 4=Occasionally 5=Regularly

| EDUCATIONAL APPROACHES | DESCRIPTION | SAMPLE PROGRAMS/EVENTS | PRESCHOOL CHILDREN | YOUTH | ADULTS | SPECIAL GROUPS | OTHER |
|---|---|---|---|---|---|---|---|
| Religious Instruction | Understanding "about" things; comprehension about concepts under study | Sunday School Bible study Topical course | | | | | |
| Dialogical Learning | Structured intentional process for understanding, insight, and application | Bible or book study Support group | N/A | | | | |
| Praxis-Reflection | Learning through guided experiences and through reflection and action | Missions experiences Ministry experience Retreats | | | | | |
| Training | Acquiring skills and moving toward increased mastery | Ushering Teaching Tech support Ministries Workshops | | | | | |
| Sponsorship | Reciprocal relationship of encouragement and introduction or induction into community | Baptisms Programs Groups (support, etc.) | N/A | | | | |

| Method | Description | Examples/Setting | | | | | |
|---|---|---|---|---|---|---|---|
| Apprenticeship | Learning in relationship from and alongside an expert | | | | | | |
| Mentoring | A bounded learning vocational relationship whose purpose it is to introduce people into vocational work or fields | Any vocational setting | N/A | N/A | | | |
| Small Groups | Learning in the context of a group of persons (4–18 persons) with common interests and high accountability to a mutual interest | Bible study Support group Book study Fellowship | N/A | | | | |
| Intergenerational | Learning in a communal context in which everyone, of all ages, learns the same thing at the same time together | Primarily in any corporate gathering of communal practices VBS and other intergenerational programs | | | | | |
| Retreats | An extended (two days to a week), off-site, experientially structured or unstructured time for reflection, study, or sharing; a retreat is not a glorified workshop—its focus is on gaining perspective, discernment, relaxation, recreation, refocusing, gaining insight, etc. | Spirituality retreat Writing retreat Men's retreat Women's retreat | | | | | |
| Learning through obedience | The stance and practice of putting faith in action, which assumes that insight and learning follow the act of obedience; "obey to learn" rather than "learn to obey" | Ministries Service projects Spiritual direction Mission trips and events Spiritual disciplines | | | | | |

# 6

# Planning Centered on the
# Christian Church Year

Planning the curriculum of the congregation is the heart of the work and ministry of the CELT. Planning flounders when congregations lack a framework that informs the goals of the education program, the values of the faith community, or the theological purpose of educating in faith. The final result can be a curriculum that becomes no more than an aimless hodgepodge of activities, disconnected events, and a schedule full of competing programs. The reality is that all experiences of congregational life are formative. However, as educator Dean Blevins points out, "The collective interplay of all the domains may result in either a deliberate formative life or an eclectic dissipation of confusing, contradictory practices."[1] The goal of planning for Christian education formation is not to fill the calendar with activities; rather, it is the programming of those experiences that will help people grow in faith in the context of a community of faith.

The Christian Church Year is perhaps the best framework for a community-of-faith approach to planning the Christian education formation ministry of the church. The curriculum of the church has more to do with how we structure communal life than with what often is referred to as curriculum—namely, printed resources ordered from publishing houses. As Veverka emphasized, "Congregations educate by the way they organize and structure their life and work. The primary 'curriculum' of Christian education is the life and activity of the local church."[2] Robert K. Martin stresses, "It is important to realize that the primary responsibility of church leadership is to cultivate these hidden...dimensions of ecclesial life that are already present in congregations."[3]

## Educating for Faith in Community

In chapter 2 we explored the concept that a congregation is an authentic community of faith. Often we fail to appreciate the treasure that lies in the uniqueness of church as community. Educating for faith in that context requires a different kind of learning and a different way of thinking about, and practicing, teaching, learning, and curriculum development. Charles R. Foster stated, "Perhaps the most powerful of all gifts to the world found in the Christian heritage is its sense of community. Its promises confront the messages of fragmentation and violence dominating social relationships."[4] We should strive, then, to live into the richness of being community as fully as we can in our Christian education formation planning. John Westerhoff identified eight aspects of communal life that enhance Christian formation as a basic form of discipleship:

1. Communal rites, particularly those repetitive, symbolic, and social acts that express and manifest the community's sacred narrative along with its implied faith and life;
2. The church environment, including architectural space and artifacts;
3. The marking of time, particularly the Christian Church Year calendar;
4. Shared communal life, including the polity, programs, and stewardship of life;
5. The practice of spiritual disciplines, including structured practices within the community;
6. Fellowship through social interaction via interpersonal relations and motivations;
7. The influence of role models (exemplary and mentors);
8. Language, which both reveals and shapes behavior, cultural values, and self-identity.[5]

Christians are formed in community through participation in the practices of faith, and through the experiences of the life of faith mediated by relationships. Planning for Christian education formation takes into account that for Christians in community "the organizing principle for building community emerges from their relationship to the events that give purpose and meaning to their existence."[6]

## The Christian Church Year as a Framework for Planning

A central premise of our approach for Christian education formation is that the Christian Church Year should be the foundational schema that guides the planning and practice of the congregation, including its education ministry. The phrase "Liturgical Church Year" is used in many church traditions. The word *liturgical* comes from the Greek *leitourgia,* which means "the work of the people." When the people of God follow the Christian Church Year, they are acting out the "Story of God." They are rehearsing remembrance of God's redemptive history through the Church and giving testimony to their relationship to God. Through the cyclical observance of the Christian Church Year congregations pass on the traditional practices of the historical Church to their children, to the uninitiated, and to the next generations. The seasonal events of the Christian Church Year "establish a structure for the interplay of a congregation's identification with certain paradigmatic events in our faith history and its responses over the years to local circumstances and relationships."[7]

The lectionary works in tandem with the seasonal emphases of the Christian Church Year. The lectionary is a three-year scriptural plan using selected passages from the Old and New Testaments to guide preaching and other aspects of corporate worship. Some congregations follow the lectionary precisely. Others follow the Christian Church Year but do not use the lectionary, or use a modified form of it. Using the lectionary ensures that the congregation is served a balanced diet of scriptural passages and makes the preaching, worship, and education events congruent with the seasons and emphases of the Christian Church Year. Using the lectionary for planning the Christian education formation programs helps members develop a corporate resource of biblical knowledge and of the faith.

## The Value of Using the Christian Church Year as a Framework for Planning

Three key reasons encourage us to use the Christian Church Year as a framework for education planning. First, using the Christian Church Year as a framework for planning keeps the congregation focused on its mission: to be the called people of God in the world. The lives of Christians are often influenced more by the rhythm of a secular calendar rather than the Christian Church Year. Christians struggle for ways to express and make meaning of their faith amid the noise and distractions of the post-Christian world culture in which many live and work. Using the Christian Church Year as a framework for congregational life and learning assists the congregation in knowing what it should be doing and teaching in the present moment or season. When we use the Christian Church Year as a planning tool, the Church's mission to worship God, live in obedience to God, and participate in God's work of love and reconciliation is kept at the center of congregational life.

When the Christian Church Year is not the framework for Christian living that guides our practices of faith, we find it harder to keep God at the center of our lives. Our sense of calling and mission then becomes clouded by the influences of secular life. Simply stated, the Christian Church Year frames our purpose for existence and our relationship to God and others. It helps us discern our Christian calling and to live in obedience to God guided by a clear understanding of ways to practice our Christian faith. The observance of the rhythms of a distinctly Christian cycle shapes our Christian identity.

Second, the Christian Church Year provides a practical thematic approach for congregational life and learning. Using the Christian Church Year as a framework for planning leads to the integration of congregational events and activities resulting in shared formative experiences. The result of such integration produces a Christian community that understands its corporate identity and need for interdependence as the body of Christ. The Christian Church Year contains themes that provide guidance for the development, or choice, of education resource literature for all ages. These themes form the content of our faith that arises from scripture and tells the Christian Story. Planning around the Christian Church Year can help the CELT choose education literature that coincides with a balanced study of scripture. It also frames the scope and sequence of study materials that are inclusive of Christian history, Christian practices, and church polity.

Third, using the Christian Church Year as a framework for planning helps create an environment for effective faith formation. Because a congregation is a community of faith, and its relationships mediate spiritual formation, congregations must challenge structures and programs that promote a fragmented education ministry that segregates the congregation by age-graded events and promotes an individualistic and privatized understanding and approach to faith formation. We are formed in community, not apart from it. The Christian Church Year helps promote the course of the entire life of the church as the congregation's curriculum for educating persons in faith in a communal context. Using the Christian Church Year as a planning tool helps form the congregation into a community where persons can encounter the faith and learn its lifestyle. The life of the community becomes the practice of faith.

### Liabilities of Not Following the Christian Church Year

Foster identified four tasks pertinent to building community in a pluralistic world: "(1) transmitting the vocabulary of Christian faith; (2) sharing the stories of faith; (3) nurturing interdependent relationships; and (4) practicing the life-style of Christian community."[8] If the church fails to teach the members of our community of faith how to "pay attention" to life and living by helping them structure their lives with Christian intentionality, then someone else will. For better or worse, most of our church members mark the rhythms of life and cycles of time by a secular calendar. Perhaps this is why so many Christians today find it difficult to make meaning of their lives in day-to-day living. For example, Advent should be a time of penitence, preparation, anticipation, and reflection. However, for most Christians the secular pattern of scurrying around in a panic, fighting traffic, standing in long lines, and spending money on things they do not need is overt evidence of what is going on in their inner lives during that season of the Christian Church Year.

When I was growing up, our community customarily reserved Wednesday evenings and Sundays for church events. Over time, the secular influence of sporting events encroached upon church activities. Today, on any given Sunday, many parents have to choose between church and whatever seasonal sport is being played. Many church people are more likely to take the kids to the ball field than to church! Consider the following chart that contrasts the Christian Church Year with the secular calendar year. If we are honest, we will confess that the lives of most of our church members are structured more around the events and values of the secular calendar year than from a Christian orientation. Little wonder that their faith is not an integral part of daily living.

### Figure 6-1: Contrasting the Christian Church Year with the Secular Calendar Year

| CHRISTIAN CHURCH YEAR | SECULAR CALENDAR YEAR |
|---|---|
| Advent | New Year's Eve and Day parties |
| Christmas/Christmastide | Winter blockbuster movies season |
| Epiphany | Hockey season |
| Ordinary Time | Superbowl Sunday |
| Baptism of our Lord | "Winter holiday" |
| Transfiguration Sunday | Tax season |
| Lent | Baseball spring training |
| Ash Wednesday | Golf season |
| Holy Week | Spring break |
| Palm Sunday | Vacation time (forget about church) |
| Maundy Thursday | Summer movie season |
| Good Friday | Back-to-school shopping season |
| Easter/Eastertide | Football season |
| Ascension | Basketball season |
| Pentecost | New TV season |
| Ordinary Time | Thanksgiving (Pre-Christmas shopping) |
| Trinity Sunday | Christmas shopping season |
| All Saints Day | |
| Reformation Sunday | |
| Reign of Christ (Christ the King) | |

For most Christians in our culture the secular consumerist calendar has more influence than the Christian Church Year. This is all the more reason congregations must be intentional in using the Christian Church Year as a planning tool to shape a congregational perspective toward a life centered on the life of faith. Observing the Christian Church Year puts the secular events of life into proper perspective.

### Planning Christian Education Formation around the Christian Church Year

The Christian Church Year cycle tells the Christian Story, beginning at Advent with the life of Christ from his birth through his resurrection on Easter Sunday morning, and includes yearly attention to fundamental doctrines and historical observances of the Church. Using the Christian Church Year as the framework for planning the Christian education formation ministry of the church ensures that the congregation is exposed to the full span of the Christian Story and provides balance to education planning.

## Advent

Advent (literally "coming" or "arrival") marks the beginning of the Christian Church Year and is the season of anticipation. Advent is a time of preparation for the coming of the Christ when the church highlights the theological themes of hope, redemption, and promise and teaches the doctrine of the Incarnation.

Advent offers a wonderful opportunity to teach through symbols and rituals. Using the color purple helps create the moods of penitence and preparation. To differentiate between Advent and Lent, some congregations use the color blue instead. During this season many congregations use an Advent wreath to mark time and emphasize the posture of anticipation and expectancy. The lighting of each Advent candle emphasizes the themes of hope, love, joy, and peace. Christmas Eve culminates with the lighting of the Christ candle. Additional symbols—such as the hanging of greens, poinsettias, and a Chrismon Tree filled with Christmas symbols—help highlight the meaning of the season.

## Christmastide

Christmastide begins with Christmas Day followed by eleven days through Epiphany, often referred to as "The Twelve Days of Christmas." We celebrate the joy of the birth of the Christ child during this season. The colors for this season are white and gold, representing joy and festivity. Teaching themes include thanksgiving and gratitude for God's promises, and stories about the childhood of Christ.

## Epiphany

The word *epiphany* means "manifestation" and highlights God's promise of redemption and hope in Christ as revealed and offered to the Gentiles. The celebration of this manifestation, or revealing, on January 6 highlights the biblical story of the visit of the Magi who followed the star as they searched for Jesus. The star and light are two symbols used to indicate that Jesus is the light of the world. White is the color for this day of celebration.

### Ordinary Time (Shorter Season)

The period after Epiphany and before Lent is the season of Ordinary Time. Two seasons of Ordinary Time appear during the Christian Church Year. This is the shorter season. The longer season of Ordinary Time occurs after Pentecost Sunday and completes the Christian Church Year cycle. The color for both seasons is green, representing growth in the Christian's life. During the Ordinary Time after Epiphany the church emphasizes Jesus' growth from early childhood. Two special Sundays are celebrated during this short season–the Baptism of Our Lord, recalling Christ's baptism and wilderness experience, and Transfiguration Sunday, which recalls Jesus' transfiguration on the mountain with Elijah and Moses. White is the color for these two special days.

### Lent

The season of Lent begins with Ash Wednesday and continues for forty days prior to Easter, not counting Sundays. The forty days of Lent echo Jesus' forty days of wilderness preparation for ministry after his baptism. Lent is a time for penitence and preparation for Easter. Ash Wednesday marks the beginning of this penitential period by focusing on the themes of sin, death, and repentance. Ashes are a biblical symbol of repentance and often are imposed in the form of a cross on the foreheads of the penitent as a sign of confession and repentance.

Lent was historically a time of preparation for new converts in anticipation of their baptism at Easter. Over centuries it has become a time of reflection and self-examination in preparation for Easter Sunday. The color purple is used during Lent. Crosses are often draped in a purple cloth. The Lenten season offers an opportunity for focused education programming related to the observance of spiritual disciplines, starting new small group Bible studies, and offering Lenten studies related to the themes of the life of Christ: death and hope, healing, prayer, and spiritual disciplines.

### Holy Week

The final week of Lent is Holy Week. It begins on Palm Sunday, recalling Jesus' triumphant entry into Jerusalem. Maundy Thursday or "command" Thursday focuses on Jesus' words on the night of his Last Supper with them: "I give you a new commandment, that you love one another. Just as I have loved you, you also should love one another" (Jn. 13:34, NRSV). Maundy Thursday worship often includes communion and sometimes foot washing as a reenactment of Jesus' last meal with his disciples. The paraments and decorations are often removed from the sanctuary on this evening in preparation for Good Friday, the day commemorating Christ's crucifixion, death, and entombment. Many churches will focus on Jesus' experience on the cross through the seven last words of Christ. Crosses often are draped in black on this day to symbolize Jesus' death.

### Easter and Eastertide

The Easter season–called Eastertide or the Great Fifty Days– begins at sunset on Easter Eve and continues through the Day of Pentecost. Easter Sunday is the most holy day of the Christian Church Year, the culmination of the hope of the Church and the affirmation of Christ as Lord through resurrection. The colors for this season are white and gold, symbolizing royalty, purity, and joy. The Paschal candle, a large white candle, is lighted throughout the Easter season symbolizing Jesus Christ, the Paschal Lamb. On the fortieth day after Easter, the Church celebrates Ascension Sunday, commemorating Christ's ascension into heaven.

### Pentecost

Pentecost is the fiftieth day after Easter. Tongues of fire are the traditional symbols of Pentecost, symbolizing the giving of the Holy Spirit to Christ's followers and the birth of the Church. The traditional color for Pentecost is red, representative of the tongues of fire (the Holy Spirit) that came upon the gathered disciples. This is an ideal time to teach about, and celebrate, the nature and mission of the Church, and about one's particular church as a body of believers who make up part of the body of Christ, and about the enduring presence of God in our midst.

### Ordinary Time (Longer Season)

The period of time following Pentecost is called Ordinary Time (also referred to as Kingdomtide). This is the second and longer period of Ordinary Time when the Church places emphasis on Christian growth. Education themes focus on the life and teachings of Christ, the kingdom of God, the nature of the Church, and the disciplines of the Christian life. The color is green, which symbolizes growth.

Four special days in the life of the Church are celebrated during Ordinary Time. Trinity Sunday (white) teaches about the doctrine of the Trinity. All Saints' Day (white) is a time of remembrance of the saints of the Church who have gone before us. In Protestant congregations Reformation Sunday (red) commemorates the Protestant Reformation, and Christ the King Sunday (white) is the last Sunday of the Christian year. On this Sunday the church celebrates and proclaims the reign of Jesus Christ.

The following chart shows how a CELT may plan for education formation using the Christian Church Year as a foundation for planning. The programs and events on the chart are merely examples of possibilities for planning. There is no single right interpretation of the practices and programming of the themes during the Christian Church Year. Your CELT will determine how best to shape its ministry using the Christian Church Year, taking into consideration the church's congregational identity and culture and its understanding of its mission.

Figure 6-2: The Christian Year and Education Formation Themes

| CHURCH YEAR | CONGREGATIONAL THEMES | MONTHS OF THE YEAR | SAMPLE PROGRAMS AND EVENTS |
|---|---|---|---|
| Advent | Incarnation<br>Anticipation<br>Penitence<br>Preparation<br>Refection<br>Hope<br>Love<br>Joy<br>Peace | December | Advent Devotions<br>Advent Bible Studies<br>Advent Wreath<br>Benevolent Projects<br>Chrismon Tree<br>Christmas Musicals and<br>　Dramas<br>Christmas Intergenera-<br>　tional Workshop<br>Hanging of the Greens |
| Christmas<br>Christmastide | Incarnation<br>Celebration<br>Festivity<br>Joy | December | Christmas Eve Service<br>Communion<br>Twelfth Night |
| Epiphany | The Word<br>Witness<br>The Star<br>Visit of Magi<br>Light | January | Spiritual Gifts Class<br>Lessons on Epiphany<br>Outreach Emphases<br>Winter Spirituality Retreats |
| Ordinary Time<br>　(Short)<br>Baptism of Our<br>　Lord Sunday<br>Transfiguration<br>　Sunday | Baptism<br>Christian Growth<br>　and Discipleship | January-<br>February | Stewardship<br>Discipleship Study<br>Baptism Preparation Study<br>Catechetical Classes<br>Winter Bible Studies<br>Service of Baptism |

| Shrove Tuesday (Mardi Gras) Ash Wednesday Lent Holy Week Palm Sunday Maundy Thursday Good Friday | Confession Penitence Personal Assessment Repentance Death and Hope | February-March | Ash Wednesday Service Good Friday Service Lenten Studies Maundy Thursday Palm Sunday Tenebrae Service Lenten Studies |
|---|---|---|---|
| Easter Sunday Eastertide | Celebration Resurrection Victory Hope | April-May | Easter Eve Service Easter Sunday Services |
| Ascension Sunday Pentecost Sunday Trinity Sunday | The Church Faith Family Sabbath | April-May | Family Dedication, Children's Sabbath Sunday Family Retreat Marriage Retreat Parenting Workshop Intergenerational Events Youth Sunday |
| Ordinary Time (Long): World Communion Sunday Reformation Sunday All Saints' Day Thanksgiving Christ the King Sunday | Answering Our Call Growth in Faith and Discipleship Service Spirituality | June-November | All Saints Recognition Children's Camp Communion Emphasis Covenant Emphasis Diaconate Retreat Discipleship Classes Spiritual Gifts Emphases Leadership Appreciation Men's Retreat Mission Trips New Bible Study Year Prayer Emphasis Fall Promotion Sunday Spiritual Disciplines Stewardship Emphasis |

With the Christian Church Year themes in mind, the CELT can develop congregational themes for the year. Using a similar chart, a CELT may use the following process to plan for the year:

1. Identify the theological and biblical themes of the Christian Church Year;
2. Determine the themes that the congregation will emphasize;
3. Work at the intentional integration of programs, practices, and activities;

4. Set dates and times on the calendar for theme-related programs and events;

5. Publicize the yearly calendar with advance notice to the congregation.

Charles Foster emphasized the power of formative corporate events in the life of the congregation as community. He identified four kinds of events that provide a rhythmic pattern to the participation of people in communities: paradigmatic, seasonal, occasional, and unexpected. These four types of events provide the vehicle for the community of faith to be the medium for educating in faith. For example, paradigmatic and seasonal events, such as those provided by the observance of the Christian Church Year, "establish a pattern for our lives as persons and as groups. The patterns for Christian life and community have their origin in significant events deeply rooted in our ancient transitions and rituals and recounted in sacred texts and stories. These events provide a persistent structure that gives order and purpose to our common lives. They establish standards and expectations for our participation and commitments."[9]

## Program Development

Church leaders struggle with two common issues: how to determine what is successful versus what is effective, and how to interpret people's participation in events–or lack of it. Here are some basic rules that can help the CELT get a handle on planning the church education ministry.

*Persons who show up at an event are the ones who need to be there.* I am continually puzzled at the over-focus on numbers in congregations. If 100 people do not show up at an event, then the event is considered a "failure" (even when it is a congregation of only 50 people!). My own rule about education events is, "I'll work with whoever shows up"–even if it is only two people. When you plan and offer an event, the people who will attend are the people who have a felt need for what you are offering. The "other" people who you imagine "should" be there are of no consequence to the effectiveness of the event, nor to whether or not the "few" who attend get what they need. Focus on the ones who have invested their time in coming, not on the ones who did not.

*Not everything is for everybody at the same time.* As a rule, an effective program will be about *one* thing. That means the people who attend are the ones who need that *one* thing. Many people will not need or be interested in that one thing at the time you offer it. Get clear about the population you are aiming for in the program. Make sure you promote and announce what you are offering in the ways and in the venues those people need to hear it. For example, do not promote an event on parenting to people who do not have children in the home (empty nesters or couples without children). Do not promote a program on divorce to married couples. The people who are interested in the topic of divorce are those who have experienced a divorce.

*If you plan something good and no one shows up, do it again next year.* Too many church educators give up on good programs and education offerings because no one—or "too few"—showed up the first time it was offered. You spend a lot of energy to create and offer a new program and event and are disappointed when people do not "get it" the first time. People cannot appreciate what they do not know, and likely will not make a connection between a "new" program offering and what they need. If you offer a program your people need, but with limited results, offer it again the following year. Sometimes people need to "recognize" something as "familiar" before they embrace it. People need to "see" and "hear" a new message eight times before actually noticing it. In our experience, a new program generally requires three years to "take." If you have just a few participants this year, resist the temptation to cancel the event. (If you need a critical mass, announce how many you need to register for the event up front.) People need to hear those who attended the first time talk about how meaningful the experience was—word of mouth goes a long way in helping a program succeed.

*If you offer an event that meets people's needs, offer it again in three years.* Surprisingly, educators too often think of an event as a "one-shot deal"—even when it is well-received, meets people's needs, and gets great feedback. Some people who needed that event were not able to participate for some reason—they will benefit from it being offered again. Another group of people—especially families—did not need what you offered this year—but in three years they will be at a different place and will need it then. All those families with only preschoolers at home will not have attended this year's program related to children in the family—but in three years, those preschoolers will be "children" and those same parents will need and want that event. When you discover a good program that meets the needs of people, put it on the calendar for three years down the line. You'll reach a whole group of people who did not need it now, but will need it then.

*When programming, focus on people's needs and not their predilections.* "Interest" is not a sufficient enough motivator for learning or change. An unrealized or perceived need is a motivator. Focus on offering those programs that will give the most return on your investment of time and effort. People "want" a lot of things–and some people just want to be entertained. However, people already have enough entertainment in their lives. (Don't believe it? Consider how much money your congregational members spend on "entertainment" in comparison to how much they give to missions or to the church.) Entertainment is such an overwhelming element in people's lives that many of them live trivial lives without realizing it. Feeling "affirmed" feels good, but it does not lead to growth or maturation. Challenge is more effective than cuddling when you want to help people grow. And the goal of education is, after all, growth.

*When planning an event, ask, "What's the theology that informs this?"* Christian education must always be undergirded by an informing theology. A Christian theology that frames and informs the education events at the church is what makes Christian education "Christian." If what the church offers people is not different from what society offers, why offer it? Most often, society can do it better. You need to do it for a difference.

### Avoiding Program Proliferation

Congregations often get to a stage when they are tempted to engage in a round of program proliferation. Usually, as a result of a long-range planning process, congregational surveys, or the result of a particularly enthusiastic planning retreat, a list appears of a dozen new programs various church groups think they should start within the year. Often this includes a mix of in-house programs for various populations within the congregation and of outreach to identified populations outside of the congregation. New programs will then be launched–usually under leadership of professional staff and enthusiastic and committed laypersons. The problem arises when within a few months these news programs cannot be sustained due to various factors: lack of (or competition for) funding and resources, waning interest and commitment on the part of the leaders, a lack of support from participants, a lack of integration with the larger life or schedule of the congregation.

A congregation that lacks intentional program planning will eventually wind up with the same people moving from one program to another with no gain of results in program effectiveness. The most

committed people in your congregation are already as busy as they can be participating in current programs.
Start new programs only when

- your average Sunday morning worship attendance is 200 to 350, then start a new group every two years;
- you can identify a population that has particular needs not currently met by existing programs;
- a church member feels called to a particular ministry that does not duplicate what current programs are doing and meets a need, then encourage and facilitate that new ministry's success.

Have patience. Know it takes about two to three years for a new program to "take," so do not make attendance the gauge for success.
Close out existing programs when they are

- floundering
- stuck on a plateau
- ineffective

Realize that every program will have its own life span. Rather than trying to resuscitate programs, allow them to atrophy. Put your energy in creating a new program to take their place or in other programs obviously meeting people's needs.
In a congregation with average Sunday morning worship attendance of 350 to 500, you should maintain a balance in the ratio of programs focused for in-house ministries and those that provide opportunities for ministries outside of the congregation. Starting at the 500 mark, you should strive for a 2-to-1 ratio (two *outside* ministry programs or groups to every one in-house program or group).
Before starting new programs and ministries, do a program audit. Determine:

- How many programs (classes, groups, ministries, etc.) currently are running?
- How many attend and participate in these programs?
- How many nonmembers or prospective members participate in these programs?
- Which population groups participate (and which do not)?
- How well are the programs funded?
- Where and when do they meet?
- How effective and stable is the leadership for these programs?

Take these guidelines into consideration when starting a new program. If you make no adjustment to the ministries or programs budget or do not increase the level of resources, leadership development, or support, you run the risk of shortchanging all existing programs for the sake of the new, untried one. To determine if your congregation is suffering from program proliferation and to check for a balance in programs for age groups, use the Year-at-a-Glance worksheet at the end of this chapter.

## Avoiding the Danger of Myopic Content

One value of the Christian Church Year approach to planning is that it ensures a balanced exposure to the corpus of the Christian faith. The cyclical revisiting of major themes and doctrines of the faith is a corrective to a myopic overemphasis on one facet of belief, doctrines, or of Scripture. This dynamic can be helpful in addressing the tendency of some study groups to develop the unhealthy pattern of relying on study materials from a single publisher or a particular popular or esoteric author. Without proper guidance, these study groups may choose study materials that do not comply with the values, general spirit, and teachings of the congregation or the larger Christian tradition. Using the Christian Church Year as a planning framework, the CELT can assist small group leaders in choosing materials that protect them from overexposure to one author's (often narrow) views and ensure that the study experiences of small groups are congruent with the theology, identity, and values of the congregation.

## Conclusion

The CELT should use the Christian Church Year as the framework to guide the life and work of planning events and programs. In this way the team can tap into one of the most formative ways that faith is shaped in a community-of-faith environment. The Christian Church Year will provide a framework in which the biblical narrative may be lived out in congregational experience and practice. It will help the CELT pay attention to the emphases of the Christian Story so that they may lead the congregation to experience the full Christian Story of faith in study and practice.

Using the Christian Church Year offers many opportunities for educating in faith using the arts, visuals, and symbols. The Spirit resides in the affect (feelings, emotions, and intuition). Providing for educational aesthetics helps cultivate a theology of the heart in balance with a theology of the mind. Most importantly, using the

Christian Church Year cycle as a foundation for planning will provide the integration necessary for effective education formation to occur through participation in the course of the life of the church, which is, after all, the real curriculum of faith. The fundamental principle for educating in faith is that the practice of Christian disciplines is the method for acquiring them. It is the task of the CELT to cultivate, with informed intentionality, the life of faith of the community of faith. As Foster stated, "Community does not just happen. It requires the commitment and effort of its members to intend that its future shall be maintained and renewed through subsequent generations."[10]

**Figure 6-3: Year-at-a-Glance Christian Education Programming Calendar Assessment**

| January | | February | | March | |
|---|---|---|---|---|---|
| No. of children's events: | | No. of children's events: | | No. of children's events: | |
| No. of Youth events: | | No. of Youth events: | | No. of Youth events: | |
| No. of Adult events: | | No. of Adult events: | | No. of Adult events: | |
| No. of Special groups: | | No. of Special groups: | | No. of Special groups: | |
| No. of seasonal events: | | No. of seasonal events: | | No. of seasonal events: | |
| No. of outreach events: | | No. of outreach events: | | No. of outreach events: | |
| No. intergenerational: | | No. intergenerational: | | No. intergenerational: | |

| April | | May | | June | |
|---|---|---|---|---|---|
| No. of children's events: | | No. of children's events: | | No. of children's events: | |
| No. of Youth events: | | No. of Youth events: | | No. of Youth events: | |
| No. of Adult events: | | No. of Adult events: | | No. of Adult events: | |
| No. of Special groups: | | No. of Special groups: | | No. of Special groups: | |
| No. of seasonal events: | | No. of seasonal events: | | No. of seasonal events: | |
| No. of outreach events: | | No. of outreach events: | | No. of outreach events: | |
| No. intergenerational: | | No. intergenerational: | | No. intergenerational: | |

| July | | August | | September | |
|---|---|---|---|---|---|
| No. of children's events: | | No. of children's events: | | No. of children's events: | |
| No. of Youth events: | | No. of Youth events: | | No. of Youth events: | |
| No. of Adult events: | | No. of Adult events: | | No. of Adult events: | |
| No. of Special groups: | | No. of Special groups: | | No. of Special groups: | |
| No. of seasonal events: | | No. of seasonal events: | | No. of seasonal events: | |
| No. of outreach events: | | No. of outreach events: | | No. of outreach events: | |
| No. intergenerational: | | No. intergenerational: | | No. intergenerational: | |

| October | | November | | December | |
|---|---|---|---|---|---|
| No. of children's events: | | No. of children's events: | | No. of children's events: | |
| No. of Youth events: | | No. of Youth events: | | No. of Youth events: | |
| No. of Adult events: | | No. of Adult events: | | No. of Adult events: | |
| No. of Special groups: | | No. of Special groups: | | No. of Special groups: | |
| No. of seasonal events: | | No. of seasonal events: | | No. of seasonal events: | |
| No. of outreach events: | | No. of outreach events: | | No. of outreach events: | |
| No. intergenerational: | | No. intergenerational: | | No. intergenerational: | |

# PART III: Operation of Planning

*Implementation of Plans for a
Christian Faith Community*

# 7

# Assessing Effectiveness

Until we stop engaging in "pretend schooling" in our churches' education enterprise, we will never be effective in our efforts. I offered this challenge during a Christian education conference for pastors, congregational staff, and lay leaders. "Pretend schooling" involves building education buildings, setting up classrooms, equipping them with education paraphernalia, purchasing education materials, assigning a teacher, populating the classroom with "students," and then going through the motions of doing "education" things, such as taking attendance. Rarely does our congregational Christian education engage in the actual practice of applying education processes to our education programs.

Hearing that challenge, a responsible pastor asked for an example of education practices that congregations tend to ignore. I provided two basic examples. First, rigorous education practice calls for the construction of well-designed global program goals and specific learning objectives. Second, sound education practice calls for assessment of effectiveness and learning based on those goals and objectives.

I asked, "How many of your congregations have written goals for your education programs?" In a room of two hundred people, not one raised a hand.

Then I asked, "How many of you write out specific learning objectives when you prepare a lesson you'll teach at church?" Again, no one raised a hand.

"How many of your congregations engage in regular, ongoing teacher training and then do annual teacher performance reviews?" No hands.

Finally, I asked, "How many of your congregations engage in evaluation processes to verify that your church members are growing in the faith and learning what you want them to learn in your education enterprises?" Seeing that again no one raised a hand, I said, "That's what I mean by pretend schooling."

The claim that much of what passes for Christian education in churches is "pretend schooling" is not a new insight. Over eighty years ago educator George Herbert Betts claimed:

> Anomalous as it may seem, the Sunday School has not, in the vast majority of churches, for approximately the last hundred years of its history in the United States, been definitely *educational* in its aims or program. Its primary purpose in the minds of many, if not most, of its promoters in the evangelical churches is that of conversional evangelism, the fundamentally educational aspect of its work being secondary.[1]

Congregations that want to provide an effective education program that makes a difference in the lives of the participants need to move beyond going through the motions of a "pretend school" and actually engage in sound educational practices and processes. Regardless of the context in which learning happens—a school, college, or community—educational processes must be applied to the practices of educational planning, organization, and delivery. This chapter will provide a beginning framework for assessing your Christian education formation program. By the time you conclude this chapter, you will have an idea about what to assess, when to assess, and how to assess your education program.

## The Purpose of Assessment

The purpose of engaging in ongoing formative assessment is twofold. First, we want to assess how effective our education programs and activities are. We invest a lot of time, resources, and energy in our education programs. It is important to know, then, whether what we are doing is making a difference, and to what extent. If we say that participation in Christian education formation is important for the spiritual growth of our congregational members and vital to the health of our churches, then we need to support that claim beyond mere talk.

Second, by engaging in formative assessment, we can uncover areas of the church education formation programs where change is needed. A well-designed assessment of our education programs can help us determine what kind of changes we need to make to be more effective, and when we need to make them.

The assessment process merely helps answer the basic questions your CELT should be continually asking: What are we trying to accomplish? How well are we doing it? How can we improve what we are doing and the manner in which we carry it out? How, and in what ways, do our programs actually help our members grow in their faith and ministries? The key question you want to answer as a result of your assessment is: How effective is our Christian education formation program? That, in turn, raises the question: "What is effectiveness? Effectiveness is simply how congruent the results of your activities, programs, and efforts are with the goals, intent, and purpose of your program. If the intent of your Christian education formation program is to help church members grow in their spiritual lives, then you should have evidence they actually are growing. If the goal of your Sunday school program is to help the participants grow in their understanding of the Bible, then you should be able to describe the type of new understanding members actually have gained.

Effectiveness also involves how well your Christian education formation program is informed by, and applies, sound educational practices and theory. For example, how closely do the components of your congregation's Christian education formation program give attention to the developmental dynamics of how adults, children, preschoolers, and youth grow in faith? How closely does your program give attention to the corporate dynamics of church as a community of faith? How closely are the stated outcomes, goals, and objectives of your education programs related to biblical mandates about making disciples? How effectively do you match educational content with appropriate educational approaches?

## What Should We Assess?

What you assess will depend on what you want to discover and what you want to improve. You can assess any of the several components of your congregational education program. For example, you can assess the results of your programs based on their stated goals. Or, you can assess the process you use for planning and designing your education programs. You can choose to assess your processes and practices for recruiting teachers and workers, or your training programs for teachers and leaders. You can assess the level of satisfaction with education programs of your church members or their perception about facets of your church programs. More mundane, but no less important, you can assess your education programs' impact on your facilities and physical plant. In other words, you can assess almost anything! The important question to consider, however, is "What is most worth assessing and for what purposes?" In the end your assessments should lead to decisions and action. Therefore you want to resist investing time and effort in assessing something that, despite the results of your evaluation, you will not change.

To determine what you need to assess, consider what level of assessment is needed. Since properly done assessments can be complex and time consuming, you should choose only one level and dimension of assessment at a time. Once you decide on the level of assessment, you want to stay within its scope. The following chart can serve as a guide to pinpoint your options about the level of assessment and its scope.

### Figure 7-1: Levels of Assessment and Their Scope

| LEVEL | SCOPE OF ASSESSMENT (examples) |
|---|---|
| Administrative | The planning process |
| | Supervision process |
| | Administrative structures |
| | Budgeting processes and allocations |
| | The physical plant (use, impact, needs) |
| Organizational | Size of organization |
| | Structure of organization |
| | Type of organization |
| | Oversight of organization |
| | Learning environments |
| Programmatic | Types of programs |
| | Scope of programs |
| | Location of programs (at church, off-site) |
| | Goals of programs |

| Pedagogical | Teacher effectiveness |
| --- | --- |
| | Learner participation and growth |
| | Course design or program model |
| | Scope and sequence of studies |
| | Curricular resources (quality, use, congruence with goals) |
| | Learning contexts and sites (classrooms, facilities, resources) |

## Areas of Assessment

As you can see from the examples on the chart, your CELT has no end to the options for what it can assess. You will want to choose to assess those areas that address current issues related to your education program's effectiveness. Assessment needs to be relevant to your current needs. Sometimes, it is helpful to determine what you need to assess by posing a "discovery question." Choose a level of assessment (administrative, organizational, programmatic, or pedagogical) and raise a question within its scope. Your discovery question should be interesting as well as relevant. A well-articulated discovery question will help you discern what needs to be assessed.

Examples of discovery questions that fall under the scope of some broader levels of concern include:

### *Assessing Facilities*

- Are the current facilities adequate for our existing programs?
- Are the current facilities adequate for growth?
- Are the facilities maintained adequately for safety?
- Are the facilities in compliance with local regulations?
- Are classrooms and meeting rooms adequately furnished for their use?
- Are the facilities handicap-accessible?
- Are the facilities kept attractive and clean?
- Is the budget sufficient for regular maintenance?
- Is there effective oversight of the facilities?
- Do our facilities enable and enhance the capacity to function as a community of faith?
- Are our facilities assigned properly according to the physical and numerical needs of the various age groups (senior adults not on the top floor; growing children's classes not crunched into the smallest classrooms)?

### *Assessing Program Development*

- Are the programs informed by clear, published goals and objectives?
- Are the programs consistent with the mission and vision of the congregation?
- Are the curricular resources used in the programs congruent with our congregation's values and theological beliefs?
- Are the curricular resources used in the programs congruent with, and do they foster, a community-of-faith approach to learning?
- Is there an effective process in place for program development?
- Is our education budget sufficient for maintaining current programs and developing future programs?
- Is the scope of the education program sufficient for the needs of members?
- Do we have policies in place that adequately govern and address current issues, processes, and structures?
- Are there gaps in the populations served by our programs?
- Do the church education programs meet the needs of those for whom they are designed?
- How effective is our discipleship process in providing spiritual growth opportunities to our congregation?
- Do our programs reflect our biblical values in content and approach?
- Do our programs enable and enhance the congregation's capacity to function as a community of faith?
- Do we have programs we should close down because they no longer meet the needs of the intended audience?

### *Assessment of Teachers and Faculty*

- Do we have an effective process in place for teacher recruitment?
- Do we have an effective program for teacher and faculty development?
- Do we provide adequate training for the teachers and workers?
- Do we have a satisfactory level of participation at teacher training programs?
- Do we have adequate numbers of teachers for all programs?
- Do we have published ministry (job) descriptions to help guide the teachers?

- Are we in compliance with child protection policies for screening teachers and volunteers?
- Are teachers knowledgeable about the Bible?
- Are teachers knowledgeable about age group faith development?
- Are teachers knowledgeable about age group characteristics?
- Do our teachers demonstrate commitment to the ministry of teaching?
- Do teachers demonstrate spiritual maturity and commitment to their growth?
- Do our teachers appreciate and foster the value of and commitment to being a community of faith?
- Do our teachers seek to know and meet needs of their students?

### *Assessment of Organization and Structure*

- Do we have policies and procedures in place that provide adequate guidelines for practice?
- Do we have policies and procedures in place that facilitate sound and responsible decision-making?
- Is our organization sufficient for coverage of necessary tasks?
- Do we have sufficient leaders for our organizational structure?
- Are our leaders well trained for their work?
- Is the organization bloated and inefficient?
- Is the structure of the organization congruent with the task and mission?
- Does the organization facilitate ministry effectiveness, or is it an obstacle?
- Is the Christian education formation ministry sufficiently funded?
- Does our organization facilitate and enhance our ability to be a community of faith?

### The Assessment Process

The assessment process is not complex, but it should be followed rigorously. Each step is an important part of the process, and each is interrelated to the whole. Effective assessment processes are circular. They "close the loop" by starting and ending with your program goals. Specifically, begin your assessment process by defining the goals of your Christian education formation program, and then complete the process by evaluating and revising your program goals as necessary. (See Figure 7-2.)

Figure 7-2: Assessment Process

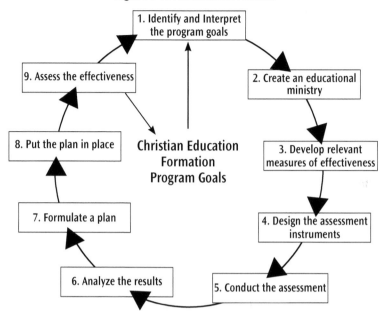

Here are the steps to an effective assessment process.

1. *Identify and interpret the goals of your Christian education formation program,* including program outcomes and desired student learning or type of growth. If this is your congregation's first attempt at assessing your Christian education formation program, you may be surprised to discover that you may not be able to find any existing program goals. If that is the case, then the first step in the assessment process is to define the goals of your program. This in itself can become a long process of study and discernment. Consider the importance of completing this step: without clearly stated program goals, how can you know what you are trying to accomplish? How can you determine whether or not you are doing it well or at all?

2. *Create an education ministry curriculum inventory.* Once you identify the goals of your Christian education formation program, create a curriculum inventory of your Christian education ministries. Make your inventory as comprehensive as you can. You can use whatever approach works best for you: a calendar map on which you list all the education programs and events for the year; a scope and sequence of

concepts and Bible content; your purchased curricular products; an inventory listing by age-graded ministries (adults, preschool, children, youth, etc.) and interest groups (young adults, young families, singles, support groups, etc.); or an inventory by programs (Sunday school, Bible studies, adult classes, retreats, training, etc.).

Include in your inventory those indicators of effectiveness you think are most important and that will add value to your assessment. For example, you can include the number of faculty and education leaders involved; the number of education hours for each event or program, the number of participants; the cost of maintaining each program (materials, etc.); the effectiveness of persons who have oversight for the programs; the space requirement for programs; the specific audience who participates; the participants' travel time to the church; a listing of members, prospects, and visitors who participate; a listing of length of church membership tenure of the participants; etc.

To create a more comprehensive Christian education formation program inventory related to church life as curriculum, examine a year's worth of your church's newsletter, bulletin, or calendar. Remember that "everything we do is Christian education," and that the curriculum of your church consists of its corporate practices of teaching (*didache*), worship (*leitourgia*), community (*koinonia*), proclamation (*kerygma*), and service (*diakonia*).[2] Or, put another way, Christian education is "all those relationships and experiences which are offered to individuals and groups as they participate actively in the life of a congregation."[3]

3. *Develop relevant measures of effectiveness.* This third step of the process may be the most challenging. To be of genuine value, your assessment of ministry program effectiveness must be able to assess valid measures of effectiveness. This step will require some study to identify and adopt valid and realistic measures of effectiveness. You will need to identify appropriate measures for the level you want to assess: administrative, organizational, programmatic, and pedagogical. (See Figure 7-1 on pages 101–102.) You can find printed standards for these levels in various places. Check your denomination's education ministry services for recommendations and resources.

4. *Design the assessment instruments.* Once you have determined the relevant measures for effectiveness, you need to design your assessment instrument. A number of types of assessment instruments are available, but you will need to choose the one that best fits with what you are trying to assess and what you are trying to discover. Some

of the assessment methods you can use are: surveys, questionnaires, interviews, audits, observational methods, standardized tests, institutional data, consultations, the case study method, focus groups, and an advisory committee. You may wish to use a combination of these methods depending on your assessment needs.[4]

5. *Conduct the assessment.* Once you have identified your goals, determined your standards for effectiveness, and designed your assessment instruments, you are ready to conduct the assessment. To get the best results, be sure you seek the information you need from the appropriate sources. If you want to survey attitudes about Sunday school, then survey those members who attend Sunday school. It does not help to solicit opinions about the effectiveness of your Sunday school from persons who do not attend. If you want to understand the obstacles to participating in Sunday school, or discover the reasons people do not attend, then survey those who do not participate in Sunday school. For churchwide surveys, make every effort to get as many responses as you can. Mailing the survey to the membership, or as an insert in your church newsletters, are two methods. Another is to administer the survey before or after a worship service. (Realize, however, that not every member is present during any one service. The typical worship attendance pattern in most congregations is that most of your members will attend church at least once or twice a month. That means that administering a survey on one Sunday morning service runs the risk of missing a significant portion of the congregation.) Typically you will provide a deadline for the information-gathering phases. Make sure you give people enough time to respond to a survey before the deadline. Likewise, give yourself enough time to engage in other information-gathering activities (audits, examining records, interviews, panels, etc.). Once you arrive at your deadline for gathering information, you should not extend this stage of the process. Move on to the next step in the process.

6. *Analyze the results.* Once you've collected your data or information, you need to analyze and interpret the results. This step involves determining if and how the data answers the questions you were asking. Analyzing the data may also yield new questions. Ultimately, this step culminates in an interpretation of what the data or information demonstrates and recommendations for action based on that interpretation. Analyzing the data involves asking a new set of questions: Did you gain sufficient information or data to answer your discovery questions? Are there gaps in the information or data

that leave you unable to answer a question or make an observation? Can you discern patterns or trends? Is your data quantifiable (numerical or statistical), or is it qualitative (opinions, perceptions, and perspectives)? Can you summarize the information or data? Can you make recommendations for action based on the data or information?

7. *Formulate a plan for change and improvement.* Your interpretation of the data will guide you toward the action steps you need to take. Use your interpretation of the assessment results to make plans for improving your Christian education formation program. Your plan for improvement should address those areas you have identified as needing attention. Resist the temptation to make changes in areas that your assessment did not cover and for which you have no data for interpretation.

8. *Put your plan in place, monitor the effects of the change, and adjust the plan as necessary.* Your plan should be designed to facilitate the changes necessary to increase your programs' effectiveness. Once you put your plan in place, monitor the effects of how the changes you have put in place are affecting your programs. No plan is perfect, so anticipate that you will need to adjust the plan along the way. Be flexible as you tweak the plan. Keep tweaking until you are satisfied that you can begin to see the improvements you are looking for.

9. *Assess the effectiveness of the plan.* The planning process does not end until you "close the loop." "Closing the loop" involves returning to your starting point (your program goals or your discovery questions) and determining how your plan informs, challenges, or changes it. Give your plan enough time to develop and to be in effect long enough to have a chance to work. When appropriate, assess the effectiveness of the plan. You can do this by repeating the original assessment process (repeat the original survey, for example), or you can devise a different assessment tool to determine whether or not your plan is yielding the improvement results you were looking for.

## Characteristics of Effective Assessments

Practicing sound education assessment may seem like an over-whelming project, especially if your congregation is not in the habit of doing it on a regular basis. But assessment is a necessary practice if you are serious about providing an effective education formation program that makes a difference in the lives of your members. You will find that, once you complete the first round of an assessment process, it becomes less daunting.

As you plan to conduct your assessment process, keep in mind these characteristics of effective assessment:

• *A system that is easy to understand.* Your CELT will likely rotate members. New members need to be able to quickly understand the reasons, nature, and process for performing assessments. The more complex your system for assessment, the less likely your leadership team members will be able, or willing, to follow it. Keep it simple.

• *A system with manageable components.* Recall the classic advice on how to eat an elephant: one small piece at a time. Similarly, your assessment system should be able to be completed by doing one step at a time.

• *A system with a minimal administrative workload for leadership team members.* Your CELT members should be more involved with the planning and analysis process than with administration. Choose a person that is gifted in the "grunt work" of administrative processes (even if you need to get a person outside the committee) and free your team leaders to do the creative work. Often, getting a "project manager" to give administrative oversight to a major assessment project helps make for an efficient and effective experience.

• *A system that makes it easy to conduct assessments, conduct reviews, and to submit assessment plans and results.* The harder it is for your team leaders to complete each step, the more obstacles you will have to hinder the process.

• *A system that produces useful results.*

• *A system that is worth the effort of your leadership team.* While you want to make assessments a matter of routine in the sense that they are a regular part of the education administration of your programs, they need to have a purpose and add value to the ministry. Assessments that do not go anywhere or do not result in plans for improving effectiveness are a meaningless activity. Before long, if they do not see its value, your leadership team will cease to participate in the important work of formative assessment.

## A Model for Formative Assessment

Assessment works best when it is ongoing rather than sporadic. The most effective assessment processes are formative rather than reactive. In other words, including assessment of your ministry effectiveness as part of the regular work of your leadership team is more effective than cranking out a survey as an anxious response to complaints or when things have gotten so bad that programs are "broken" because of neglect. Formative assessment will help ensure qualitative developmental improvement toward a more effective Christian education formation ministry. That means that your Christian education formation programs will always be getting better, rather than suffering from stagnation and neglect for lack of attention. Ongoing formative assessment also helps ensure that we are responsible stewards of the calling and charge to make disciples of Christ who are maturing, growing, and participating fully in the life of the body of Christ.

An effective way to institute your Christian education formation assessment is to use a three-year cycle model for formative assessment that is easy to begin and easy to maintain. You will want to begin by instilling in your leadership committee the value of, and commitment to, formative assessment. Then, provide the training they will need to carry out the process effectively. For your first three-year cycle you may begin modestly, then increase the complexity and extent of your assessment as you become more competent and confident about the process.

### First Year

On the first year of your formative assessment process, offer an orientation and training for the assessment process and procedures to your team leadership. One result of your preparation for the training should be the development of a resource manual for the process. You will continue to develop the manual over the first three-year cycle. Beginning to create this resource at the start will help you avoid having to reinvent the wheel each year. You can use the material in this chapter as a starting point for the content of your assessment resource manual. Plan on scheduling an assessment training event every three years as part of the leadership development component of your Christian education formation program—in most cases, churches will rotate committee or team members every three years, so this practice will help ensure everyone is aware and on board. Make the training available to other groups in the church who need to implement an assessment.

Once your CELT is trained, begin the formative assessment by concentrating on one area of your ministry. We recommend that you begin with the preschool and children's education ministries. If your education programs for each of those age-group ministries are large, then conduct separate assessments for each. Your ministry coordinators on the leadership team should lead the assessment process along with the church staff, the chair and co-chair, the project manager if you use one, and with the help of the other leadership team members.

Remember that being part of a team means that no one works as a Lone Ranger in carrying out any aspect of the ministry, such as assessments. Only by working together can all members of the CELT ensure that the assessment will give attention to the integrated and interdependent education needs of the community of faith and avoid an over-focus on isolated aspects or groups in the church. In this first year the CELT will conduct the assessment of preschool and children's ministries.

### Second Year

During the second year the CELT, under the guidance of the preschool and children's ministry coordinator, begins to make plans for improving effectiveness based on the results of the assessment. The planning process will give attention to those areas assessed and will call for decisions about organization, recruitment, scheduling, budgeting, and programming as needed. Also during the second year the team will begin the assessment of the youth ministry area under the direction of the youth ministries coordinator with the help and support of the staff, chair and co-chair, and the other members of the education leadership team.

### Third Year

By your third year the assessment process is in full swing. As per the chart "Education Programs Assessment Schedule" on page 113 in year three the preschool and/or children's ministry coordinator will implement the plan created in year two. Meanwhile, the youth ministries coordinator will begin the work of formulating the plan informed by the results of the assessment conducted the previous year. Year three is also the time to begin assessment of the congregation's adult Christian education formation programs. Leading this is the adult ministries coordinator, with the help and support of the committee as a whole, the staff, chair, co-chair, and the other members of the congregation as necessary.

Unless you have an additional coordinator on the leadership team for specialized ministries, any evaluations related to specialized education ministries are conducted this year under the direction of the chair and co-chair. Specialized ministries may include support groups, interest ministries (divorce recovery, etc.), and special population programs (deaf ministries, homebound ministries, etc.). It will become important to determine which ministries are appropriate for the CELT to take responsibility for. One way to approach that issue is to ask the question of each congregational ministry, "Where does this ministry belong, and who is responsible for it?" Programs and ministries that lack clear connections to the larger part of the church often lose effectiveness, lack accountability, lose their direction, flounder, and drain resources.

### *Fourth, Fifth, and Sixth Years*

During the fourth, fifth and sixth years the formative assessment process will have become a regular part of the work of the leadership team. The preschool and children's ministries will have completed the first three-year cycle of the assessment process and implemented the plan to increase effectiveness. The fourth year will call for an in-depth summary evaluation and report of the plan's effectiveness. That year also is the time to identify the next phase or area for a formal assessment related to the preschool and children's ministry. This marks the beginning of the second cycle of assessment for the preschool and children's ministry. Because you are engaged in ongoing formative assessment, the focus of the assessment and plan for any given year will never need to be comprehensive and overwhelming. Discernment about the level and scope of the assessment (see chart 1 earlier in the chapter) will help the leadership team keep the process manageable and relevant.

During the fourth, fifth and sixth years the youth and adult ministries areas, under the guidance of the coordinators and the leadership team, continue their assessment processes. By the time the sixth year comes around, the youth Christian education ministry will be ready for their next phase of assessment, and the adult Christian education formation ministries will follow the schedule in stride.

Adopting this model means that your CELT will always be working on improving your church's education programs through formative assessment. No ministry area is ever neglected, and the staggered ongoing schedule of the assessment process will facilitate and ensure integration between the ministry program areas. When we fail to practice ongoing formative assessment, things tend to devolve in effectiveness to the point of frustration. We get the sense that everything is "broken." When that happens, the temptation is to engage in a comprehensive assessment of everything, followed by an attempt to fix everything at once. This is overwhelming and ultimately ineffective.

Because the three-year evaluation plan is formative and ongoing, the nature of the assessments will be narrower in focus and, therefore, manageable. Your CELT will focus on particular, rather than global, assessments of selected components of the education programs. Every assessment year, your team will focus on the area that needs greatest attention, assess that *one* component, devise a plan, then implement the plan to address the issues identified.

### Figure 7-3: Education Programs Assessment Schedule

| MINISTRY/ YEAR | 1 | 2 | 3 | 4 | 5 | 6 | 7 |
|---|---|---|---|---|---|---|---|
| Preschool/ Children | Conduct Assessment | Create the Plan | Implement the Plan | Evaluate and Report; Conduct New Assessment | (continue) | | |
| Youth | | Conduct Assessment | Create the Plan | Implement | Evaluate and Report; Conduct New Assessment | (continue) | |
| Adults/ Other ministries | | | Conduct Assessment | Create the Plan | Implement | Evaluate and Report; Conduct New Assessment | (continue) |

## Conclusion

The ministry of Christian education formation is one of the most important in the life of the congregation. We are called to make disciples—to help the members of our faith community grow in faith into the likenesses of Christ. It is not worthy of that calling to settle for going through the motions of playing "pretend school." Christian education in a community of faith needs to be practiced as rigorously and authentically as in any other field where the practice of education is offered. That means that education leaders must practice those processes that facilitate effective education assessment to evaluate how well we are doing what we say we are doing: helping people grow in Christ in the community of faith.

# 8

# Making the Change toward a Community-of-Faith Approach for Christian Education Formation

Making the change toward a community-of-faith approach for Christian education formation begins with a vision and a dream. If you have caught the vision for what this approach can do for your congregation, then it is time to move from envisioning what can be to making the change toward realizing the dream. A congregation that wishes to make the change toward a community-of-faith approach to Christian education formation will need to reorganize its education leadership structure.

Your congregation likely already has some sort of committee or team structure in place that guides the education ministries, or some aspects of it. You may have several faithful and committed members who have been given, or who have taken on, the responsibility for leading various programs. One challenge will involve getting those people who are already doing the work to appreciate and embrace a new way of working *together*. The change process must start with a "testing the waters" stage to begin shaping the congregational culture and its practices. Given the unsettling nature of change, you and your leaders will do well to accept the idea that the kind of changes you are seeking will require at least three to six years of ongoing planning and work by the CELT.

## Steps for Implementation

This length of time is necessary to influence cultural change in the congregation. Remember that you are striving for more than just organizational or administrative change. You are striving for a change in vision, values, and cultural practices. That kind of change takes time. If your goal for your congregation is for a more authentic way of educating in faith, the price is commitment to the task and the will to see it through.

### *Testing the Waters Stage*

Larry Osborne writes that leaders of change must sell the vision to individuals before attempting to work with groups.[1] Presenting proposals to the entire church first, contends Osborne, runs the risk of guaranteeing the rejection of any new idea. First, initial responses to new ideas are often negative due to the natural reactivity to change. Second, those negative first impressions often are difficult to overcome. Once people hear negative comments to a new idea, changing their perception becomes a challenge. Discussing an idea for change with individuals first makes it easier for people to change their minds. Plus, they become partners in educating others about how they feel about the change. According to Osborne, "Those who study the process of change inform us that only about 15 percent will adopt a new idea without first knowing who else is supporting it."[2]

The purpose of what Osborne refers to as a "test the waters"[3] phase is to discover the reactions and opinions from individual members of the congregation, not to elicit a decision for support. Testing the waters with key individuals in the congregation at the beginning of the change process helps you know if your dissatisfaction with the status quo is shared by others. It also helps you discern what aspects of the suggested change will cause the most resistance. Change always brings about anxiety, but anxiety is not a bad thing.

No one in his or her right mind jumps into a bathtub without first checking the temperature of the water. Leaders who want to initiate change need to test the waters and listen and respond to supporters and resisters as an initial step toward change. This stage will help determine if the congregation is ready and willing to embrace change. Testing the waters needs to be completed initially by the pastor, the church staff, and the congregational leaders before any plan for implementation is developed. It is imperative for the pastor and church leaders to be clear about, and supportive of, the new community-of-faith educational approach. The process will fail if the pastor is not supportive of this approach to Christian education formation. Once discernment is reached about when it is appropriate to proceed, the staff conceptualization stage can begin.

### Staff Conceptualization Stage

It is a disservice to the congregation, and risky, to form the CELT without first building a proper foundation that will ensure its success. The church staff must understand why a central CELT is necessary, what its purpose is, what authority it will have in congregational life, how it will be organized, how it will relate to the existing organizations of the church, and what implementation process is necessary to build congregational ownership.

The pastor or staff may ask other key church staff members to read this book during the "testing the waters" phase. Once that phase is complete, the staff team should schedule meetings over a two-month period to conceptualize this approach to Christian education formation, become clear about the process of change, plan the remaining months of the implementation stage, determine how each staff member will engage in the implementation process, and commit to one another in support of the process.

The pastor may lead the implementation stage or ask the resident Christian educator or an associate to lead the process. The size of your congregation may determine this. Regardless, the pastor must be engaged by demonstrating his or her support throughout the implementation process. The pastor must communicate the idea for change with organizational leaders and key groups of the congregation, and, later, with all the members of the congregation.

### The Implementation Stage

The process of implementing a planning approach using a CELT will require about an eighteen-month time period. Change takes time. The congregation will need time to learn about and process the information regarding the proposed change. According to Osborne, it is helpful to meet with small groups before making larger formal congregational presentations. Large group settings have a tendency to silence introverts and inhibit candor. Formal presentations also cause people to think they are being asked for approval rather than for their opinion.[4]

## Steps for Change

The following eight-step process is one way a congregation may begin to change its organization, culture, and practices of Christian education. Regardless of when the process begins, the launch date for ministry implementation of this new approach to planning for Christian education should coincide with the launch of the new church year. Depending on your church situation, your "new year" may be the beginning of Advent, or in the fall coinciding with a traditional academic schedule.

### Step 1: Presentation to Existing Organizational Leadership

Once the staff team understands the need for a change toward a community-of-faith education approach and is united in support of the need for a CELT, the lay leaders of the congregation's organizations must be introduced to the intended change. Throughout the process, talk about the change as a "proposed change" until the congregation formally adopts the change.

In the early stages of this process it is best to work with individuals or small groups. The staff may decide to hold a series of meetings with various organizations of the congregation—such as deacons, Sunday School and small groups leaders, missions leaders, music and worship leaders, and committee members. One advantage of this approach is that each group will raise questions from their ministry perspective. Another is that the small group approach results in more active participation because it is easier for more leaders to be engaged in the dialogue. A four-month period is needed to provide adequate time to meet with various small groups.

The purpose of these meetings is to educate toward understanding so that the leaders of the congregation will appreciate the need for change and take ownership of the upcoming process. Specifically, these leaders need to learn the details of the remaining stages of the implementation phase, the function of the CELT, and how the change will impact the life and ministries of the congregation.

### Step 2: Presentation to the Congregation

The second step is to provide information sessions for the members of the congregation to learn about the proposed change in the education ministry organization. Choose a time when most of the members of the congregation are available. The meeting should begin with an overview of the new education approach and include the following components:

1. How the idea for change came about,
2. Why this change is important for the congregation,
3. What the process has involved to date, and

4. What will occur during the remaining steps of the implementation process.

Provide time for the members of the congregation to ask questions. Publish a schedule for future opportunities for the congregational members to formulate their questions, reflect on the proposed change, and share their input in the next step.

### Step 3: Congregational Reflection and Input through Dialogue Sessions

The congregation must have a voice in the plan for change. It is a mistake to assume that the congregation will readily endorse the proposed change. In fact, congregational support for changes of this nature is so critical that it is best to table the plan if the congregation does not take ownership of the intended change. There is greater danger in proceeding without proper support than in delaying action until the congregation is ready. Step 3 allows members to share their ideas and express their concerns. They need to hear the opinions of persons who resist the change and the thoughts of those who are in support of the idea. Most importantly, members need to understand why this change is important. Allow at least three months for this work with the congregation. Make every effort to ensure that the congregation understands the need for the change and how it will impact congregational life. Expect some heightened anxiety during this time, and consider it a natural congregational reaction during this phase of the process.

### Step 4: Formal Adoption of the Education Approach by the Congregation

Marking times of meaningful transitions in the life of the community is important for a congregation. When significant shifts in practice occur, they can be nodal events during which a community of faith begins a new trajectory in its journey. These moments in time help the congregation clarify its identity, redefine what it stands for, and change how it goes about its practice of ministry. The emotional health of the congregation is enhanced when it is clear about its identity and purpose for ministry. Step 4 of the change process can serve as a watershed event that unites the congregation in its purpose.

Leaders should determine if a brief presentation of the education plan can be helpful before the formal adoption by vote, acclamation, or consensus. The presentation can review the following key concepts:

- What it means to be a community of faith,
- How the CELT will function,
- How the team will be organized,
- How leaders will be chosen for the team, and
- A summary of the remaining steps of the implementation process.

After this brief presentation, the congregation should be given time to ask questions. Then, a formal affirmation in favor of the change will be called for.

### *Step 5: Enlistment of the Christian Education Leadership Team*

Since the CELT will give overall guidance to the entire education life of the congregation, it is important for this team to consist of some of the best leaders in the congregation. Most of the leaders of the CELT are probably already serving in leadership positions that match the functions of the team. For example, the Sunday School Coordinator is likely already in place and will simply become a part of the Christian Education Leadership Team. During this step of the process, the primary purpose is to bring individuals together into one leadership group. The church staff will take the lead in suggesting leaders for this team if the congregation does not have persons serving in the coordinator positions that make up the CELT.

### *Step 6: Training the Christian Education Leadership Team*

The next step in the implementation process is to train the CELT. This training and orientation phase, which can take up to four months, is vitally important. The effectiveness of the Christian education ministry of the congregation is related to how well the team members are trained to understand their tasks and to work together as a team. A full day or overnight training retreat and additional training sessions will help team members bond. Training should cover the following areas:

- How to run and participate in effective meetings,
- Planning to use the Christian Church Year,
- Expectations of team members,
- Functions of team members,
- The three-year planning and assessment cycle,
- The team's relationship to the church organizations,
- The budgeting process and fiscal procedures, and
- The importance and purpose of the annual planning retreat.

Initial training needs to focus on issues of clarity and function. The team must understand its purpose. Each member must understand what he or she brings to the table. "Hands-on" folks may resist this part of the training process. They want to get to work, not talk about work. Do not let enthusiasm for getting started sidestep this essential step in the process. Make it clear to team members that training will be ongoing throughout the year as the team faithfully carries out its work.

### Step 7: The Development of a Yearly Planning Calendar

Having received its initial training, the CELT can begin its work by developing the yearly planning calendar. The team should plan only the major education events and programs of the church during the first year. In subsequent years, the CELT will have more time to work with the organizations of the congregation to provide a more detailed schedule based on the Christian Church Year and informed by the culture of the church community. Eventually, the CELT will plan the ministry three years in advance.

### Step 8: The Ongoing Work of the Christian Education Leadership Team: Year One

The first year will be a formational and training period for the CELT. It will take at least a year for the team to learn to work together and to become comfortable with its function and place in leadership in congregational life. In the course of the first year the team will begin to develop a "Christian Education Manual" (if one exists it will need to be revised and updated), begin assessing the Christian education program, and make preparations for planning the three-year assessment cycle with a primary focus on the preschool and/or children's ministry. During this first year the team will monitor the cycles and rhythm of church life and will observe and assess how all aspects of congregational life are balanced and integrated so as to address education formation programming needs.

### A New Way of Educating in Faith

In her study of vibrant congregations, Bass concluded, "The congregations studied have found new vitality (viability, spiritual depth, renewed identity and mission, and, often, numerical growth) through an intentional and reflexive engagement with Christian tradition as embodied in the practices of faith, with the goal of knowing God."[5]

## Figure 8-1: Making the Change to Education Formation

| STAGES | ISSUES ADDRESSED | DURATION | DETAILS OF PROCESS |
|---|---|---|---|
| Testing the Waters Stage | Sharing concept with individuals Vision casting Dissatisfactions, Resistances, & anxiety Eliciting reactions & opinions, not seeking decisions for support at this stage | 4 Months | Sharing details of new education approach to: • Pastor • Individual Staff Members • Key Church Leaders • Staff as a Team |
| GO or NO GO Decision | | | |
| Staff Conceptualization Stage | Staff gets clear about process and implementation stage | 2 Months | Staff teambuilding and planning in support of new education approach |
| Implementation Stage: | Groups Involved: | 18 months | Educating Small Groups and Congregation & Steps to Implementation |
| Step 1 | Small Leadership Groups | 4 months | Presentation to Existing Organizational Leadership: • Deacons • SS Leaders •Music & Missions leaders •Committee Leaders •Etc. |
| Step 2 | Congregational Banquet | Special Event (next month) | Presentation to Congregation |
| Step 3 | Congregation | Town Hall Type Group Sessions for 3 Months | Congregation Reflection & Input Through Dialogue Sessions |
| Step 4 | Congregational Business Meeting | Special Event (next month) | Formal Adoption by Congregation |
| Step 5 | Church Staff & Nominating Committee | 2 Months | Enlistment of C.E.L.T |
| Step 6 | C.E.L.T. | 4 Months | Training of C.E.L.T |
| Step 7 | C.E.L.T. | 3 Months | Development of Yearly Planning Calendar & Its Promotion |
| Step 8 | C.E.L.T. | New Education Process Begins | C.E.L.T. Launch Date: First year of C.E.L.T. work begins: Development of CE Manual and Assessment of CE Program |

The community-of-faith approach to planning for and practicing Christian education will change congregational life, resulting in new vitality, spiritual growth, and renewed identity in the community of faith. Any congregation that lives into this educational approach will be characterized by these practices:

- Enlisting and empowering a central CELT that will guide the education life of the church;
- Focusing on the Christian Church Year as a basis for planning the education formation programs of the church;
- Placing greater emphasis on the integration of all aspects of congregational life by seeking ways to bring the congregation together as community rather than segregating for isolated activities;
- Seeking or developing literature that engages all ages and groups in the same theological themes as a way to enhance spiritual conversation at church and at home, and that fosters a corporate and communal understanding of Christian identity;
- Allowing children of all ages to participate in worship rather than isolate them from corporate worship for "pretend" or "play" worship training;
- Viewing the worship and music ministries of the congregation as part of the education curriculum of the congregation and inviting the CELT to have input into worship and music planning, as appropriate;
- Seeking ways to emphasize the importance of corporate worship in community as a key formation experience for all of the members;
- Making every attempt to plan congregational ministries and activities that are authentically Christian in nature and clearly support the mission of the congregation;
- Encouraging an experiential approach to faith formation by engaging members of the congregation in education ministries and missional events beyond the church building;
- Developing an intentional process of Christian calling, Christian vocation, and gifts discernment;
- Partnering with and assisting parents in making the home a primary place for spiritual learning and nurturing;
- Recognizing the importance of the faith community in early childhood Christian education and its implications for faith development;

- Providing opportunities for members of the faith community to share their stories and make meaning of their experiences of life and faith through reflection and sharing;
- Making the practice of spiritual disciplines a primary education method that will enable the grace of God to work in the lives of the members;
- Fostering small groups ministry as a primary approach for educating in faith.

These examples reflect ways to practice Christian education that support a holistic understanding of the way faith is formed in a community of faith. These values and practices must become an overt part of the communication and planning process of the CELT.

## Conclusion

The answer to the question, "Is a congregation a school or a community of faith?" will determine how a congregation goes about its planning and what practices it provides that form and transform the lives of its members. This is the watershed question that will tilt congregational practice toward effectiveness or ineffectiveness. The decision regarding this question will impact congregational life. Any congregation involved in evaluation and visioning must address this question to become clear about its educational philosophy. In our opinion, evidence is clear that an exclusive schooling approach to Christian education is not sufficient and that congregations must use approaches that are congruent with how faith is formed in a community of faith to provide effective faith formation.

We believe that God's Spirit is speaking–that we are being called to a way to educate in faith that is congruent with how faith is formed in a community of faith. The first step in responding to God's call is the recognition that the way we currently practice Christian education is not the best way, and that there is a way that is more effective precisely because it is more congruent with how faith is actually formed in communities. Two paths lie before you and your congregation. One path is more of the same; the other offers the promise of new purpose and new life. Which path will your congregation choose?

# APPENDIX 1

# Community-of-Faith Approach Education Formation Assessment Planning Tool

Use this tool to assess the education formation values that influence your congregation's educational planning process. Place a checkmark next to the statements that are true of your congregation. Use this tool for discussion and planning.

### Building Community

\_\_\_\_ 1. Communal events are planned that help members of the congregation build relationships with one another.

\_\_\_\_ 2. Frequent intergenerational experiences are provided for members of all ages to learn together and from each other.

\_\_\_\_ 3. Frequent opportunities are planned and provided for members to share their faith stories.

\_\_\_\_ 4. Events are planned that help members of the congregation welcome and build relationships with persons who are not church members.

### Leadership Training

\_\_\_\_ 1. Annual leadership training is provided for all leaders of the congregation.

\_\_\_\_ 2. There is a well-functioning training coordinator who plans and provides training opportunities as needed.

### Missions & Ministry

\_\_\_\_ 1. Educational opportunities and events are planned that involve members of the congregation in local community and missions ministry.

## Organizational

_____ 1. A central Christian Education Leadership Team plans and guides the educational life and ministries of the entire church community.

_____ 2. The Christian Church Year is used as a planning guide for congregational practice.

_____ 3. All planning actions consider the values of congregational cooperation, collaboration, and communication.

_____ 4. The planning process strives for balance and integration.

_____ 5. The planning process intentionally seeks to provide a broad repertoire of educational approaches.

## Spiritual Growth

_____ 1. Opportunities to practice the classical spiritual disciplines are planned and provided for the members of the congregation.

_____ 2. Retreats are planned and offered as a regular approach for Christian education formation.

_____ 3. The children's and youth ministries focus on helping parents nurture the spiritual growth of their children and their families.

## Small Groups

_____ 1. Small-group learning opportunities are provided for members of the congregation.

## Worship

_____ 1. Corporate worship is a primary formative and educational communal practice.

_____ 2. Children participate in the entire worship service with their families.

_____ 3. Children and youth participate in worship leadership.

## Scoring

Count the checkmarks and compare to the scale below.

### Scale

15–18   Your congregation is doing an excellent job planning for a community-of-faith approach to Christian education formation

9–14   Your congregation is doing a good job of planning for a community-of-faith approach but there is room to grow

6–8   Your congregation needs to change more of its planning practices toward a community-of-faith approach to Christian education formation

1–5   Your congregation's educational planning does not reflect a community-of-faith approach to Christian education formation

# APPENDIX 2

# Sample Table of Contents for a Christian Education Policy Manual

## Christian Education Formation Goals

Infants Formation Goals (birth to 1 year)
Preschool Formation Goals (Ages 2 to 3)
Preschool Formation Goals (Ages 3 to 5, not in Kindergarten)
Preschooler Formation Goals (Ages 5 to 6)
Children's Formation Goals (Grades 1-3)
Children's Formation Goals (Grades 4-6)
Youth Formation Goals (Grades 7-8)
Youth Formation Goals (Grades 9-12)
Adult Formation Goals (Young Adults)
Adult Formation Goals (Middle-aged Adults)
Adult Formation Goals (Senior Adults)
Special Groups Formation Goals
Special Programs Formation Goals

## Christian Education Policies, Procedures, and Guidelines

Child Protection Policy
Children's Sermon Guidelines
Teacher and Volunteer Workers Enlistment Procedures
Equipment and Supplies
Permission Forms
Facilities and Room Use Policies
Classroom Decorating Policy
Spiritual Qualifications of Leaders
Teacher and Faculty Resignations Procedure
Check Requisition Policy

## Christian Education Leadership Team

Purpose Statement
Christian Education Mission Statement
Christian Education Formation Theology Statement

Christian Education Leadership Team Organization Chart
Christian Education Leadership Team Member Ministry
Descriptions
Terms of Office for Leadership Positions
The Annual Planning Retreat
Assessment Policy, Procedures, and Resources
Christian Education Newsletters Policies
Christian Education Planning Calendar
Curriculum Evaluation Policies and Procedures
Education Formation Approaches Chart
Monthly Meeting Agendas

## General Information

Church Covenant
New Member's Class
Sunday School Classes Descriptions
Map of Church and Educational Facility

## Christian Education Program(s) Budget

## Responsibilities and Duties of Program Leaders

## General

Preschool Ministry Teachers and Volunteers
Children's Ministry Teachers and Volunteers
Children's Camp Director
Vacation Bible School Director
Summer Programs Director
Youth Ministry Teachers and Volunteers
Adult Ministry Teachers and Volunteers

# APPENDIX 3

# Christian Education Leadership Team Meeting Agenda

## CHRISTIAN EDUCATION LEADERSHIP TEAM
### Meeting Agenda

| MEETING DETAILS | | ATTENDEES | | |
|---|---|---|---|---|
| Location | | ☐ CELT Chair | ☐ CELT Co-Chair | ☐ Staff Liaison |
| Date | | ☐ PMT Coordinator | ☐ CMT Coordinator | ☐ YMT Coordinator |
| Time | | ☐ AMT Coordinator | ☐ SS Coordinator | ☐ Training Coordinator |
| **MEETING HANDOUTS** | | ☐ Childcare coordinator | ☐ Member or Guest | ☐ Member or Guest |
| | | **Dates for Church Calendar & Items for Newsletter or Website** | | |
| | | 1. | 2. | |
| | | 3. | 4. | |
| | | 5. | 6. | |

| Agenda Items | Discussed | Decisions and Actions | Assigned to: | Due Date: |
|---|---|---|---|---|
| Prayer and review of minutes and issues from last meeting | | | | |
| 1. Review and assessment of previous month's events | ☐ | | | |
| 2. Reports from coordinators (plans for next month's events) | ☐ | | | |
| 3. Formative assessment reports (if needed) | ☐ | | | |
| 4. Budget review (if needed) | ☐ | | | |
| 5. | ☐ | | | |
| 6. | ☐ | | | |
| 7. | ☐ | | | |
| 8. | ☐ | | | |
| 9. | ☐ | | | |
| **Items for Next Agenda:** | | | | |
| **Date of Next Meeting:** | | | | |
| Meeting Adjournment | | | | |

# Notes

## Introduction

[1]Maria Harris, *Fashion Me a People: Curriculum in the Church* (Louisville: Westminster/John Knox Press, 1989).

[2]Morton Kelsey, *Can Christians Be Educated?* comp. and ed. Harold William Burgess (Birmingham, Al.: Religious Education Press, 1977), 9.

[3]Thomas H. Groome, "Advice to Beginners—And to Myself," *Religious Education*, vol. 102, no. 4 (Fall 2007): 365.

## Chapter 1: A Community-of-Faith Approach to Christian Education Formation

[1]Robert K. Martin, "Education and the Liturgical Life of the Church," *Religious Education*, vol. 98, no. 1 (2003): 46.

[2]Peter L. Benson and Carolyn H. Elkin, *Effective Christian Education: A National Study of Protestant Congregations: A Summary Report on Faith, Loyalty, and Congregational Life* (Minneapolis: Search Institute, March 1990).

[3]Ibid., 2.

[4]Martin, "Education and the Liturgical Life," 47.

[5]This contrasting schema first appeared in Israel Galindo, *The Craft of Christian Teaching* (Valley Forge, Pa.: Judson Press, 1998).

[6]Padraic O'Hare, "Educating for Devotion and Inquiry," *Religious Education*, vol. 76, no. 5 (Sep-Oct 1981): 509.

[7]Martin, "Education and the Liturgical Life," 59.

[8]See Israel Galindo, *How To Be the Best Christian Study Group Leader* (Valley Forge, Pa.: Judson Press, 2006) for a fuller treatment of the deficits and liabilities of the teaching-by-telling approach.

[9]Martin, "Education and the Liturgical Life," 59–60.

[10]Ibid., 44.

[11]Dean G. Blevins, "Educating the Liturgical Self: A Sacramental View of Pedagogy," *Journal of Christian Education*, vol. 45, no. 3 (December 2002): 14.

[12]Daniel Ciobotea, "Spiritual Theological Formation Through the Liturgical Life of the Church," *Ministerial Formation* 47 (1989): 17.

## Chapter 2: The Congregation as Community of Faith

[1]Portions of this section were originally published in Israel Galindo, *The Hidden Lives of Congregations: Understanding Church Dynamics* (Reston, Va.: Alban Institute, 1994). Used with permission.

[2]Diana Butler Bass, *Christianity for the Rest of Us: How the Neighborhood Church Is Transforming the Faith* (New York: HarperSanFrancisco, 2006), 42.

[3]Central Community Church is not the real name of the church.

[4]Robert T. O'Gorman, "The Faith Community," in *Mapping Christian Education: Approaches to Congregational Learning*, ed. Jack L. Seymour (Nashville: Abingdon Press, 1997), 50.

[5]For the concept of congregational lifespan, see Galindo, *The Hidden Life of Congregations*.

[6]Fayette Breaux Veverka, "Congregational Education: Shaping the Culture of the Local Church," *Religious Education*, vol. 92, no. 1 (Winter 1997): 80.

[7]Elizabeth Potter, "Gender and Epistemic Negotiation," in *Feminist Epistemologies*, ed. Linda Alcoff and Elizabeth Potter (New York: Routledge), 165.

[8]Wanda J. Stahl, "Congregations as the Center of Knowing: Shifting from the Individual to the Communal in Knowledge Formation," *Religious Education,* vol. 92, no. 3 (Summer 1987): 165.

[9]Portions of this section were originally published in Israel Galindo, *The Craft of Christian Teaching: How To Become a VERY Good Teacher* (Valley Forge, Pa.: Judson Press, 1998). Used by permission of Judson Press, 800–4–JUDSON, www.judsonpress.com.

[10]Maria Harris, *Fashion Me a People: Curriculum in the Church* (Louisville: Westminster/John Knox Press, 1989), 55ff.

[11]Dennis W. Foust, "Curriculum Engineering in the Local Church: A Contextual Model" (Ed.D. diss., Southern Baptist Theological Seminary, 1988), 8.

[12]Roberta M. Gilbert, *Extraordinary Relationships: A New Way of Thinking About Human Interactions* (New York: John Wiley & Sons, Inc., 1992), 3.

## Chapter 3: Organizing the Christian Education Leadership Team

[1]For a fuller treatment on how the size of a congregation affects the communal life of the congregation, see Israel Galindo, *The Hidden Life of Congregations: Understanding Church Dynamics* (Reston, Va.: Alban Institute, 1994), 77–94.

[2]Smaller congregations (with 50 to 150 average worship attendance) struggle to get enough leaders on committees or ministry teams. If yours is a smaller congregation, the "Christian Education Leadership Team" approach and organization will work if you scale down the number of persons on the team. The key to effectiveness is not the number of persons on the team; rather, it is clarity about the function of the team: planning, coordinating, and evaluating the formation education ministry of the congregation. In fact, it is easier for a smaller congregation to put this integrative model in place and grow with it than it is for a larger congregation to have to reorganize after things get fragmented.

## Chapter 4: The Work of the Christian Education Leadership Team

[1]The following resources can help you understand and discover your Christian philosophy of education: R. P. McBrien, *Basic Questions For Christian Educators* (Winona, Minn.: St. Mary's College Press, 1977); S. C. Perks, *The Christian Philosophy of Education Explained* (Whitby, England: Avant Books, 1992); L. Richards, *A Theology of Christian Education* (Grand Rapids: Zondervan Publishing House, 1975); Robert W. Pazmiño, *Foundational Issues in Christian Education* (Grand Rapids: Baker Academic, 1997); Jeff Astley, *The Philosophy of Christian Religious Education* (Birmingham, Ala: Religious Education Press, 1994); James E. Reed and Ronnie Prevost, *A History of Christian Education* (Nashville: B&H Publishing Group, 1998).

## Chapter 5: Education Formation Approaches in Congregations

[1]James Michael Lee, *The Shape of Religious Instruction: A Social Science Approach* (Birmingham, Ala.: Religious Education Press, 1971), 8.

[2]Israel Galindo, *How To Be the Best Christian Study Group Leader* (Valley Forge, Pa.: Judson Press, 2006).

[3]Edmund O'Sullivan, Amish Morrell, and Mary Ann O'Conner, *Expanding the Boundaries of Transformative Learning* (New York: Palgrave, 2002), 63.

[4]Diana Butler Bass, *Christianity for the Rest of Us: How the Neighborhood Church Is Transforming the Faith* (New York: HarperSanFrancisco, 2006), 42.

[5]Peter L. Benson and Carolyn H. Elkin, *Effective Christian Education: A National Study of Protestant Congregations: A Summary Report on Faith, Loyalty, and Congregational Life* (Minneapolis: Search Institute, March 1990).

## Chapter 6: Planning Centered on the Christian Church Year

[1]Dean G. Blevins, "Educating the Liturgical Self: A Sacramental View of Pedagogy," *Journal of Christian Education*, vol. 45, no. 3 (December 2002): 15.

[2]Fayette Breaux Veverka, "Congregational Education: Shaping the Culture of the Local Church," *Religious Education*, vol. 92, no. 1 (Winter 1997): 81.

[3]Robert K. Martin, "Education and the Liturgical Life of the Church," *Religious Education*, vol. 98, no. 1 (2003): 47.

[4]Charles R. Foster, *Educating Congregations: The Future of Christian Education* (Nashville: Abingdon Press, 1994), 56.

[5]John Westerhoff, "Fashioning Christians in Our Day," in *Schooling Christians: 'Holy Experiments' in American Education*, ed. Stanley Hauerwas and John Westerhoff (Grand Rapids: William B. Eerdmans, 1992), 262–81.

[6]Foster, *Educating Congregations,* 68.

[7]Ibid., 45.

[8]Ibid., 68.

[9]Ibid., 43–44.

[10]Ibid., 68.

## Chapter 7: Assessing Effectiveness

[1]George Herbert Betts, *The Curriculum of Religious Education* (Whitefish Mont.: Kessinger Publications, 2006), 34. Betts' book was originally published by Abingdon Press in 1924.

[2]Maria Harris, *Fashion Me a People: Curriculum in the Church* (Louisville: Westminster/John Knox Press, 1989), 55ff.

[3]Dennis W. Foust, "Curriculum Engineering in the Local Church: A Contextual Model" (Ed.D. diss., Southern Baptist Theological Seminary, 1988), 8.

[4]For a good resource on congregational assessment with a listing of options in methods, see C. Jeff Woods, *User Friendly Evaluation: Improving the work of pastors, programs, and laity* (Herndon, Va.:Alban, 1995). For a thorough step-by-step treatment on using surveys in the congregational setting, see Leon McKenzie, *Decision Making in Your Parish: Effective Ways to Consult the Local Church* (West Mystic, Conn.: Twenty-Third Publications, 1980). The following books are concise and accessible resources for learning how to design, conduct, and interpret surveys. David Chaudron, *Master of All You Survey* (San Diego: Organized Change Publications, 2006); Arlene Finke, *The Survey Handbook* (Thousand Oaks, Calif.: Sage Publications, 1995); Priscilla Salant and Don A. Dillman, *How To Conduct Your Own Survey* (New York: John Wiley & Sons, 1994); Lloyd Corder, *The Snapshot Survey* (Chicago: Dearborn Trade Publishing, 2006).

## Chapter 8: Making the Change toward a Community-of-Faith Approach to Christian Education Formation

[1]Larry W. Osborne, "Making Changes Without Getting People Steamed," *Leadership Magazine*, 19 (Spring 1998): 47.

[2]Ibid.

[3]Ibid., 46.

[4]Ibid., 47.

[5]Diana Butler Bass, *Christianity for the Rest of Us: How the Neighborhood Church Is Transforming the Faith* (New York: HarperSanFrancisco, 2006), 305.

# Bibliography

Astley, Jeff. *The Philosophy of Christian Religious Education*. Birmingham: Religious Education Press, 1994.

Bass, Diana Butler. *Christianity for the Rest of Us: How the Neighborhood Church Is Transforming the Faith*. New York: HarperSanFrancisco, 2006.

Benson, Peter L. and Carolyn H. Elkin. *Effective Christian Education: A National Study of Protestant Congregations: A Summary Report on Faith, Loyalty, and Congregational Life*. Minneapolis: Search Institute, March 1990.

Betts, George Herbert. *The Curriculum of Religious Education*. Whitefish, Mont.: Kessinger Publications, 2006. Originally published by Abingdon Press in 1924.

Blevins, Dean G. "Educating the Liturgical Self: A Sacramental View of Pedagogy," *Journal of Christian Education*, vol. 45, no. 3 (December 2002): 7–18.

Chaudron, David. *Master of All You Survey*. San Diego: Organized Change Publications, 2006.

Ciobotea, Daniel. "Spiritual Theological Formation Through the Liturgical Life of the Church," *Ministerial Formation* 47 (1989): 12–20.

Corder, Lloyd. *The Snapshot Survey*. Chicago: Dearborn Trade Publishing, 2006.

Finke, Arlene. *The Survey Handbook*. Thousand Oaks, Calif.: Sage Publications, 1995.

Foster, Charles R. *Educating Congregations: The Future of Christian Education*. Nashville: Abingdon Press, 1994.

Foust, Dennis W. *Curriculum Engineering in the Local Church: A Contextual Model*. Ed.D. Dissertation, Southern Baptist Theological Seminary, 1988.

Galindo, Israel. *How To Be the Best Christian Study Group Leader*. Valley Forge, Pa.: Judson Press, 2007.

____. *The Craft of Christian Teaching: How To Become a VERY Good Teacher*. Valley Forge, Pa.: Judson Press, 1998.

____. *The Hidden Lives of Congregations: Understanding Church Dynamics*. Herndon, Va.: The Alban Institute, 1994.

Gilbert, Roberta M. *Extraordinary Relationships: A New Way of Thinking About Human Interactions*. New York: John Wiley & Sons, Inc., 1992.

Groome, Thomas H. "Advice to Beginners–And to Myself." *Religious Education*, vol. 102, no. 4 (Fall 2007): 362–66.

Harris, Maria. *Fashion Me a People: Curriculum in the Church.* Louisville.: Westminster/John Knox Press, 1989.

Kelsey, Morton. *Can Christians Be Educated?* Compiled and edited by Harold William Burgess. Birmingham, Ala.: Religious Education Press, 1977.

Lee, James Michael. *The Shape of Religious Instruction: A Social Science Approach.* Birmingham, Ala.: Religious Education Press, 1971.

Martin, Robert K. "Education and the Liturgical Life of the Church." *Religious Education*, vol. 98, no. 1 (2003): 43–63.

McBrien, R. P. *Basic Questions For Christian Educators.* Winona, Minn.: St. Mary's College Press, 1977.

McKenzie, Leon. *Decision Making in Your Parish: Effective Ways to Consult the Local Church.* West Mystic, Conn.: Twenty-Third Publications, 1980.

Nelsen, C. Ellis. *Where Faith Begins.* Atlanta: John Knox Press, 1971.

O'Brien, Maureen R. "How Are Together: Educating for Group Self-Understanding in the Congregation." *Religious Education*, vol. 29, no. 3 (Summer 1987): 315–21.

O'Gorman, Robert T. *The Faith Community in Mapping Christian Education: Approaches to Congregational Learning.* Edited by Jack L. Seymour. Nashville: Abingdon Press, 1997.

O'Hare, Padraic. "Educating for Devotion and Inquiry." *Religious Education*, vol. 76, no. 5 (Sep-Oct 1981): 505–16.

Osborne, Larry W. "Making Changes Without Getting People Steamed." *Leadership Magazine,* 19 (Spring 1998): 42–48.

O'Sullivan, Edmund, Amish Morrell, and Mary Ann O'Conner. *Expanding the Boundaries of Transformative Learning.* New York: Palgrave, 2002.

Pazmiño, Robert W. *Foundational Issues in Christian Education.* Grand Rapids, Mich.: Baker Academic, 1997.

Perks, S. C. *The Christian Philosophy Of Education Explained.* Whitby, England: Avant Books, 1992.

Potter, Elizabeth. *Gender and Epistemic Negotiation in Feminist Epistemologies.* Edited by Linda Alcoff and Elizabeth Potter. New York: Routledge, 1992.

Reed, James E. and Ronnie Prevost. *A History of Christian Education.* Nashville: B&H Publishing Group, 1998.

Rendle, Gilbert R. *Leading Change in the Congregation: Spiritual and Organizational Tools for Leaders.* Herndon, Va.: The Alban Institute, 1998.

Richards, Lawrence. *A Theology of Christian Education.* Grand Rapids: Zondervan Publishing House, 1975.

Salant, Priscilla, and Don A. Dillman. *How To Conduct Your Own Survey.* New York: John Wiley & Sons, 1994.

Stahl, Wanda J. "Congregations as the Center of Knowing: Shifting from the Individual to the Communal in Knowledge Formation." *Religious Education,* vol. 92, no. 3 (Summer 1987): 298–314.

Veverka, Fayette Breaux, "Congregational Education: Shaping the Culture of the Local Church." *Religious Education,* vol. 92, no. 1 (Winter 1997): 77–90.

Westerhoff, John. "Fashioning Christians in Our Day." *Schooling Christians: "Holy Experiments" in American Education.* Edited by Stanley Hauerwas and John Westerhoff. Grand Rapids: William B. Eerdmans, 1992.

Woods, Jeff. *User Friendly Evaluation: Improving the Work of Pastors, Programs, and Laity* Herndon, Va.: Alban, 1995.

Printed and bound by PG in the USA